G000123652

0

PET[
Glas[
and [
audi[
since
Clei[
www[

[a
[r
[g
[.
[n

- Please return items before closing time
  on the last date stamped to avoid charges.
- Renew books by phoning 01305 224311 or
  online www.dorsetforyou.com/libraries
- Items may be returned to any Dorset library.
- Please note that children's books issued on
  an adult card will incur overdue charges.

Dorset County Council
Library Service

DL/2372 dd05450

Also by Peter McCarey

The Syllabary (www.knot.ch and www.thesyllabary.com)

Hugh MacDiarmid and the Russians (Edinburgh,
Scottish Academic Press, 1987)

PETER McCAREY

Collected Contraptions

CARCANET

First published in Great Britain in 2011 by
Carcanet Press Limited
Alliance House
Cross Street
Manchester M2 7AQ

A CIP catalogue record for this book is available from the British Library

ISBN 978 1 84777 073 8

The publisher acknowledges financial assistance from Arts Council England

Typeset by XL Publishing Services, Tiverton
Printed and bound in England by SRP Ltd, Exeter

FOR GRACE AND MIRTH
IN THE CITY AND STATE
OF ROSES AND RICHES
THIS GIFT

Acknowledgements

This book contains the author's poems more or less as printed in:

Town Shanties (Glasgow: Broch Books, 1991)
The Devil in the Driving Mirror (London: Vennel Press, 1995)
Double Click (Kirkcaldy: Akros, 1997)
In the Metaforest (London: Vennel Press, 2000)
Tantris (Edinburgh: *Lines Review* no.140)

Contents

TOWN SHANTIES

H$_2$O

Burning like hydrogen
blooming like gorse in a hollow, the burst
from Aber fall-pool charges the slopes
and sounds
from boulders grinding
and deeper than bones' resounding burden
of the press and turn of water
to shivers of spray in the thorn tree
standing there in broken slate
with a liverwort crust that
gleams like galena,
and each thorn glancing
with refracted fire.

Home Movie

Raindrops crowd onto the glass
in perfect silence.
Engine room noises travel up
to the eighth floor of the library
through the air conditioning system.

And this might be a nautilus
in sonar quiet
The glass – a ciné screen projection
of a flatwash and graphite Glasgow
where the frames flicker between light and lens
with the sound of steady rain.

Rain

Cats and dogs in Frosolone
pad about unheard.
Thunder, like the odd stone falling
from another roof.
The perennial rain of the rosary
makes its mark on the old women.
Ruts and runnels in chalk vennels
with water that falls again to shape
fantastic caves in the dark.

Kingdom of Light

Venafro stands in the lilac dusk
Like stones in shallow water.
Your memory submerges it
Then it floats away in its own
Electric light.

Morning Office

Morning office
Mountain glow
Cuspid ground
Sun turning
Mordant light
Mounting gold
Aqua regia
Morning glory.

Saint Magnus

The original arch is turned and reflected
on the dark glass of the mason's mind.
Aisles and tiers, as he watches,
rise and recede in the viscous light
profound and quick.

The Well-Tempered Clavier

Forty-eight angels in Leipzig
are set to cross the darkest night
in the jewels made for them
by father Bach.

Novodevichi

The Novodevichi Convent is under construction.
They are using bricks from the sixteenth century.
The walls are five metres thick, against Tartar invasion.
The frescoed visions of saints and prophets
that teemed the walls like sparrows in a hedge
are pale and peeling under the lamps:
criminals pinned to the scene of the crime
by policemen wielding the murder weapon.
They are building a cemetery of famous people
who weren't killed by Tartars.
Solovyov and Allegra
alone in the bone orchard.

Dunvegan

Celtic craft shops
Continue tradition
As maggots perpetuate
The memory of the dead.

O.E.D.

Every word in the language is laid out here
with its meaning on a tag tied round its big toe.
And here's me trying mouth to mouth.

Hogmanay

Trembling bellmetal. Standing stones
for a moment mean something.
Nothing else does.

Augrim

If gold is bezantine, gothic is blue.
Cobalts dribble from ledges,
silver in the font.
Salt waves stop in the slow lights
where coracles roll like dice.
On the ravening sea
of devoted seafarers
yours is the only quiet face.

Shipley

In drystane crannies snowflakes flock
and sheep with stain of moss and stone
on snowy fells.
Ice makes dice from dalebones.
Shivered whins are fivestanes
the sky plays.
It rocks stones,
collapses crouching arches,
in rage attacks the stellar slide
within stone,
and rugs at baffled, battled hearts.

———

Freud said, – weep,
so I can show how much I love you. –
I hate you when you cry,
mopping up with your J-cloth conscience.
Wring it out and let me get to sleep.

General Winter

Check / change down / exit / slow
ice under snow.
Sliproad slide and
the steering bridles.
Fresh fall drift
you have to dig
to find out what you used to know
Just the hush the
scurf of corky trees
collapsing crystals like collapsing trees
Snows like coalbeds consolidate
there's a road here somewhere I'll find it.

Red

And brak in roses owre a hedge o' grief
Hugh MacDiarmid

This is where the colour red enters the world
Petal-furled and nervous.
It tints green brackish, muddies in anger,
Renders despair hopeless;
Thrills in crystals, blushes in verbs.
It leaves in blood,
under the pigsty door in winter.

Glyph

Rain on a pond somehow becomes
piano improvisation
a sparrow swoops to the kerb on a cosine
dimpled air and feathered oars
the water has cut a heart shape in the rock
more even than my heart
no formula no cardioid curve
this is where proprioception
touches itself and falters
intention focuses
and burns its object sun on paper
smoke on sunlight written out
in words
in other words
to cross from see to say
is not enough
and incoherence
will catch my heel whenever I lose the way
from me to you.

Rehab No. 1 (Tennyson, to Queen Victoria)
The Victorian Queen

Rejoice, rejoice again: you hold
a higher office upon earth
than arms, or brains, or honest worth
could give the warrior queens of old.

Victorian values, futures in
the past are floated like balloons
of bakelite. A fiscal boom.
The small investor plays to win.

And should your greatness, and the care
that yokes with empire, yield you time
to make demand of modern rhyme
if aught of any worth be there;

Then – while a sweeter music wakes,
and through wild March the throstle calls,
where all about your guarded walls
the sunlit almond-blossom shakes –

I lay these verses at your feet;
for though the faults were thick as dust
in vacant chambers, I could trust
your kindness. I would be discrete.

Remember: courtly love, this cult,
this play-world in society
was counterpoised by real objection,
exposure of the 'game' as vain

and grounded in lust and appetite.
It had its serious, heavenly counterpart
in Christian devotion.
Your values have no such
collateral. The children sing:

'She wrought her voters lasting good;
her statesmen at the council met
they knew the season when to take
occasion by the wrist, and make
the bounds of freedom firmer yet

by shaping some august decree,
which kept her thrall unshaken still,
broad-based upon her party's will,
and compassed by Antarctic seas.'

Rehab No. 2 (Arnold, 'Shakespeare')

Others provide responses. You might
smile
      No comment.
The arbitrageur
who deals in sovereign states, whose pulse
powers the Dow Jones
offers the public only the public image.
You, who understood insider deals,
self-taught, litigious, more than words could wield,
walked on the earth unguessed at. Better so!
All pains the immortal spirit must endure,
all weakness that impairs, all griefs that kill
were so much grist to that fantastic mill.

Rehab No. 3 (Byron, 'Sonnet of Chillon')

Eternal spirit of the chainless mind!
In every prison freedom is a lifer
caught in the lungs then held in the heart
the heart held in by the veins it's giving blood to.

And when these men are held without parole,
without parole or civil rights to speak of,
it's just the Scottish Office tracheotomy:
what's in the wind does not go on the air.

Barlinnie, look at the years you're throwing away
like slates – denying all you might have been
and curiously proud of doing it well.

The hostage photograph, the frightened warder
this fossil forest, vaulted like the heart!
and no appeal from governor to God.

Rehab No. 4
(Pope, 'Essay on Criticism', lines 362–73)

True ease in writing came from art, not chance,
and they moved easiest who had learned to dance.
Now that I take the floor, I can't resist
giving it a good twist
Maple floorboards! Very nice
with copper nails, just like Ulysses' boat;
A sprung dancefloor. They haven't made those since
oh, since Maccaferri made guitars for Reinhardt.

But it's a foggy night.
The streetlamps, like shower nozzles
deafen, soften, dim
even the partitions of this dorm suburb.
Hung in the glassed mist, there's just
the neighbouring block
a word that's lost its tongue.

Rehab No. 5 (Milton, 'On Time')

If time is so invidious, greedy, slow,
if its values are false and vain,
its substance dross,
if it deprives us of nothing that is really ours,
then why should you plan to spend forever crowing over its corpse?
You take a madrigal and make an epitaph.
You'd end us all with your
TruthPeaceLoveJoyDeathChanceTimeHim
Who made the world and found it good.

We don't have much time
so don't waste it on heaven.
We can't live for the dead
and can only forgive them
mistakes we rehearse.
Though the lovers are one
Time passes between them.
Love stays
near undone
and reknit
like a woman in motherhood.

Rehab No. 6 (Shakespeare, Sonnet LV)

Piano tones… begin loud and bright
and then decay to silence in a complex way
that's characteristic of the instrument.

Robert Moog, *Byte* 6, 1986

Marrying clearest word to soundest verse
And five reiterations of the burden
Rowed in fire and stone (like a pharaoh's curse),
Intoned to last until the final Amen;
And we can't make head nor tail of who the song's
Regaling with its DECUS ET TUTAMEN.
Our end is nigh indeed if verse among
Stunned sinners is recalled when doom is clapping;
Absorb and sift, time, shift all that we've done,
Remit, maybe, a broken seal, Harappan
Inscription ℂ pan ↑ -ar Ɛ ki(r), 'the singer's mark',
A thunderstone. Love doesn't fear the dark.

Sous les pavés – la plage

Urban sunlight comes in the window
staggering up to its knees in sand
banknotes blowing out of its seams
like scarious leaves and carious buildings
shaking dust from my shoes but it cloys,
it clogs for I'm paid to be here.

Frontiers, harbours, roads, currencies,
crowd control and corpse disposal.

Money is busy buying itself up
using what there is for collateral.

Light is said to be sculpting itself
with its only sense
of touch.

Castle of Indolence
(Keep in a Cool Place)

First sweat dries to a crust in the breeze,
breaks up on the second, like the backwash
of a wave, pushed back on the shore by
the next one, seasick.

You leave the novel like a tepid bath
and everything's where you left it
the old iron bath of your self
with the novel and all its crew
foundering in you, your gastric juices.

I was reading like a tourist too long,
and all I wrote was like postcards home.
Now the next time I write,
you're going to turn the thing over like an
overhead cam, a mechanical stone, and say yes, but

Garden City

I dispensed the small change,
he set aside the small talk and said, 'Listen,
I'm a very good person, you know,'
which is to say: Possessions and professional
skills are not of the essence;
I am.
So I said 'Yes' and went away,
which is to say: The unsure strain of such awareness
is left to the likes of you. I want my tea.

It's good: I don't have far to go
from my refurbished close
to see the butcher's apron on a sign set
boldly in the weeping sump, the tobies and broken brick
where head-high rosebay willow herb
with clover, jaggy nettle and soothing dock
festoon and cloy the legend
WIMPEY SUPER SINGLES AND
1, 2 AND 3 BEDROOM FLATS
SELLING TO COMMENCE SHORTLY
or, in a city brasserie,
the porous tit on a plaster cast
poke out from ivy tumbling off a period cuspidor.
It's what the people want. It's what
the people who want it want. It's what the people
who want you to want it want you to want.

Elderslie

Bell the breeze, crows,
peel off the trees like burning paper
build your rafts on the highest
branches your beaks can't snap:
Sit there and crow.

Gastarbeit

It's arriving in a foreign place at night
when you don't know where to go.
You see your small self and the
compartment in the window
the luggage rack and houselights floating by
fluorescent rooms, and it enters you,
and the cold of its indifference to you
lodges like a virus in the ghettoes of your blood.

Libation Theology

A white man told his Congolese wife:
Céline says the European in Africa
disappears like a sugarlump in coffee;
she said: just so long as you stay sweet.
Quinine is bitter, though, bad medicine,
leaves the soul in chemical debt
to Prester John, Anopheles,
'venomous snake, scorching whirlwind,
neck vein swollen with anger'.
You rinse your glass with the top of the beer,
it gobs in the dust outside the bar.
You make a song to still your fear.
The jungle rises faster
than you could build a breezeblock wall.

Not Being Bob DeNiro

A colour supp. feature on Robert DeNiro –
about, more like: they could pin nothing on him.
'All our negotiations were done on the phone.'
Who pays the actor
calls the shots. It's nothing personal.
Highly professional. Bang.
And then, as Jakobson says,
To attribute the feelings expressed in a work
to the author
makes as much sense as mystery play mobs
beating up the actor who played the devil.
If you're convinced, then so am I.
The mediaeval mob is on this bus, though,
reading about someone who won't be drawn
on who calls up the demon in the cage of light.
It's us that let you command those fees;
we trade our cash for folding plush
to see you, and we want to know
just who you think you are, and what
the hell you think you're playing at.
'I want to do things that will
last because they have
substance as well as quality.'
Didn't Duns Scotus say that?
And how d'you get substance onto film?
The only substance is celluloid, – light,
if you count it as particles. Look at him there,
beating against that bright screen.
They can't even give him a definite shape.
People get so used with TV dinners
they think the packaging's what's underneath.
It gets gummed up, scar tissue to bone;
frozen or burnt to the throwaway ashet.
What's underneath this 9to5 job
that I'm trailing round like a ball and chain?
For don't you forget that as long as I loathe it,
it is not me and I am not it.
Go on, settle down to the company motor,

step on the gas of the global economy.
Money can buy you happiness (it says
in this ad for a fancy Toyota).
See if I pay just the VAT,
can I get the happiness and leave the hardware?
No? then I'll have to drag it about
and the weight of the world if need be because
I am not it and it doesn't own me.
You don't believe me. You're looking askance
or over my shoulder (get back to your crossword) –
He's got a job and a wife and a kid
and a house and a car and a notion to write.
I play golf myself; gets me some fresh air.
Great he's on xxK bloody yuppie
dinky moaning about no having time to write
because he's a wageslave.
Why doesn't he go on the broo then and write
about what it's like to be unemployed?
If I was on the dole I'd be writing, so
I wouldn't be unemployed.
I've got to come to some arrangement
and this way I still have one way out:
getting off the bus, though if I do that
then I'll soon be a stat in a government scheme.
O so he's admitting he could be worse off
after all he could be out sleeping rough
or nailing up curtains, keeping a family
on moonlight and supplementary.
That's right: this way I've got leisure to moan
so from your way of seeing it,
no right to do so. Away back to Possil.
The video van's on its way.

In the supp. there's this photo of Robert DeNiro
what's that in his jacket – a passport?
'He's Italian, he's American, he's perfect.'
I was Scottish, but British, imperfect
tense, writing not to be written out.
'Then the door flies open and he bursts in from nowhere'
So what but. What do you mean so what?

A lot of folk bought this paper;
most of them probably read this, it's
the piece with the biggest picture and fewest words.
'He was thin; his face was gaunt.
When he came back two and a half months later
he was a different man. He looks 20 years older
He's put on 30 pounds.'
Three pound a week: that's a strain on the heart.
Phantom parturition of selves
that life had left on the cuttingroom floor.
Turn time into space and lives
'll look like olive trees: pruned back
and cracked with the weight,
rerouted, culdesacked in shapes
they're not quite conscious of;
the level of sap in the lung of this tree
is conscience, me, the present tense.
The bus I'm on pulls in to the stop
and the traffic lights go to green.
Curdling smoke carved up in the headlights.
I say to myself: if we're stuck at this junction
I'll be stuck in this job for good.
The last one gets on, the lights go to red,
the bus pulls out and goes through them. So:
there'll be some hitch, some unorthodox move
to make, some rules to break, but I'll get clear.
I hadn't, actually, counted the queue,
I didn't know the sequence of the traffic lights either:
a moment's gamble it was. And yet
I did have an idea of my surroundings
and in some way this moment
shapes the next, the intellect and will.
Look into the branching light
where, stripped of substance, good and evil
can play at sticks and stones and break no bones.
'He knows it's a performance,
so he can be as villainous as the part calls for.'

Cradle

Sooner murder an infant in its cradle than nurse unacted desires
Blake, 'The Marriage of Heaven and Hell'

I

The house of death resembles the house of prayer
in simple absence of expected response
and routine presence of salaried men
who take this state of affairs as a matter of course
which of course it is.
No fingerprint on a smart professional's record.
The tonearm hangs
its table turns below
the end of the vinyl groove repeats
itself to the listening diamond
and the speakers vomit dry
a corpse is a fact a fact is a corpse
a corpse is a fact a fact is a corpse
from which we proceed to alibis
investigations and archaeologies.

A baby was strapped in his pram
on ruts of frozen mud. The woman
leaning out the window saying
was he cold? Had my wee
baby been cold? The close, cat's piss
the nasal passages long gone
with the last breath, flesh unpicked
as flotsam, carrion, greasy smoke.
To the man who has only a hammer
all the world looks like a nail.

II

Yesterday they buried six-year-old Lisa Steinberg
who had been systematically abused in her foster home,
it is suspected, by Joseph Steinberg, a middle-aged lawyer.

10 days before she died she was seen bruised and sobbing
in Steinberg's car, at a highway tollbooth.
Someone called the police,
who accepted the well-dressed lawyer's explanation.
His common-law wife, a writer of children's books,
had been beaten by her lover over a long period,
sustaining nine broken ribs, a broken jaw and broken nose.
True to 'the classic syndrome of wife battery',
she refuses to testify against him.

The child's mother, a secretary, is one respectable Roman Catholic
made pregnant by another at the age of nineteen.
Her paediatrician (now under investigation) sent her to Steinberg,
whom she paid $500 to find a good home for her baby.
'There is not one day since giving up that child
when I did not think of her,' Miss Launders said.
'If I wanted my child murdered I would have had an abortion.'

Mr Steinberg has been anxious that Lisa should have a Jewish funeral.
Lawyers fought over that request and Miss Launders won the point.
After a service yesterday conducted by a priest and a rabbi,
Lisa was being buried in the Roman Catholic Gate of Heaven
cemetery in the suburbs. The police
have found what they believe may be the murder weapon –
a rubber mallet. It does not break the skin.

With renewed purpose the police and psychiatrists
will investigate, the judges condemn
the lawyers collect, politicians deplore, priests
and columnists pontificate. In this case,
feminist criticism will be used
to restore the confidence of the professional classes.

This little death draws us like iron filings;
so many, hands black with newsprint, have come
like starlings that muster at evening on a gantry
to chatter in mutual warmth
that the girders themselves might seem to be moving, breathing.
Some social adjustment will be made
and 'the child will not have died in vain'.

III

Play back the fossil record until
scoured of every decoration. There
where semi-desert turns
the river wood to trees, erodes
the Pliocene clays, the ruts
of ancient watercourses, layers
of ash laid down in their beds,
whatever petrified bones were buried
slowly come to light and soon to dust.
Our forebears bide in the ground until
our codes are broken.
Rainprint erased from rock.
Footprints in mud that dried
3.8 million years ago
show that a pair of bipeds walked that way –
and did that hand, with gripping thumb
and buttressed fingers dandle the bone
that shivered flint
that made the axe
with which the earliest architect
struck down his wandered brother?

IV

Take my hand, give me your hand.
The mammoths fell the trees, we learn to stand.
Our fingers find, caress, command.
The hominid brain develops, and my bones
brace to contain impatient you. Just mind
the apes that rode the styptic sea
on a raft of African rainwood. Continents
and crustal plates of your skull
drift into place around them. There,
the pelvic bones unclasp, the floor gives way.

Eugene

(Sections 6, 8 and 11 of *For What It Is*)

When I was about ten years old a friend of mine told me
He said Listen Eugene
You never die in your own dream.
If you die in your own dream, you wake up dead,
He told me
That it happened to one of his uncles.
Which struck me as true, and I've always remembered it.
Well,
I died in my dream.
Not only that but the corpse was propped up
In a cage or a glass case
I kept going to look.
The eyes were still bright. I thought
Maybe they'd swivel on me
When it sensed my attention
(That seems spooky now, but in the dream it was good)
Then I came back after a couple of days
And the undertakers had been.
They'd pulled the teeth and put in dentures.
The eyes were dull, it was dead.

Rest
And gather strength
You were so nearly
Traik for the city's organ bank.

You sleep.
Dreams are secret diplomacy
Between states that you'll never know existed.
Bury your uniform in the wheat field
Let your arsenal flake in the rain.
Sleep
Don't surface yet
A sleeping conurbation
Strip light in the hospital corridor
Night light in the ward

The nurse's face is in shadow
Eugene's in darkness.

– Nurse. Nurse. Sister.
– What?
– You got five minutes?
– As it happens.
– I know what it was:
We were waiting for a train
At night in a big station.
We sat on a suitcase, we ate some cheese.
The pigeons drifted in
Down from the girders,
Along the rails;
Looked at us with one eye
And with the other eye.
One had a severed leg;
We tried to feed him, but by and by
Each one displayed it was missing a claw
Or two, tailfeathers or wing.
The bitter blind and the halt, come down
Like drops of rusty water, oil or brine
Or blood through the ceiling
Angel reptiles from aerials,
Slates and clay tiles, scaffolding
Flat roofs strung with slackwire
The frontier, slivers and spikes,
Between the conurbation and the sky
Glazed rain no mans land
Slopes and stacks diagonal
Rain rain rain rain
Bubble in the gutters and
Roan down the urban bypass
Under the asphalt.
– Eugene.
– What?
– That's five minutes.

He was out of hospital
Walking back toward his flat
It was happening again
He stopped and looked at his feet. He walked on
Toward his flat. Or maybe he should go at once
To the social. He changed direction
Name? Occupation? Reason for admission to hospital?
But there would be a queue
He thought. He'd had
A good hospital breakfast. He had
His change of clothes in his hospital bundle
A jacket, pyjamas, a bottle of limeade, a half empty
Bottle of orangeade. Shoes. Slippers.
A shaving kit – things they'd found in his house
They thought he'd want. A book with
Printed on the back 'Now and then
A novel appears that can change the
Course of your life. This is one such!'
A Western story and a detective
Story and a prayer book. Not his. Sweets and biscuits. Trousers
All in a transparent plastic bag, like
Reflecting his former life, a heavy drop.
Maybe I should go to the shops, I've nothing left for tonight.
He turned right towards the corner shop
Where they spoke Punjabi and Glaswegian. Friendly folk,
But no tick. I've no money. The bank
Did they close my current account when I went?
He stopped. Not one more step
Unless it takes me into a new life
He looked ahead. His brow,
The bough over the park paling,
The grey road led
He didn't believe it did.

Alerting

... that this book, too, has made some difference, by alerting
western students of literature to...

Victor Erlich, *Russian Formalism*

RING TALE

Ting Lear –
Ireglant
Gaeltrin
Eringalt
Relating
trigenal,
algetrin,
geanitrl:
regal nit.

Tal Niger
alerting
Ting Lear –
Tengrila
ten grail
glint. Are
near gilt,
argentli
gliteran.

Tal Niger
gent – liar:
intreagl.
Tengrila –
Tigerlan,
Grinleat.
Itler? Gna!
Atilr? Neg! –
GIANTLER,
angritel.
l...granite
graintle.

Grait nel:
Ting Lear,
nil targe,
eg train
Tengrila,
neg trail
(Irtlegan,
Geantirl,
Liartgen).

GIANTLER
Lint rage.
Ear tingl,
a-trengil,
Ting Lear –
gnat. Rile
GIANTLER.
'Ent…grail.'
'Gralient!'
'Large tin'
'Argle nit!'
'Large tin?'
'Lager tin.
Rentagil.'

Ting Lear
alert. Gin.
Gin. Alter.
Eartl gin
gin. Tra–le!
Regal Nit
leg tiran.
Lartigen!
Gin. Arlet.
Ting Lear
a–trengil.
'R, eligant'.
Rae glint;
Entragil?
Neat girl,

girt, neal.
Genitral.
Genitalr.
Galentri.
Inert gal.

entir – Alg!
GIANTLER!

Ting Lear,
great nil:
nil targe,
lager tin.
Ran gilte.
Neg trail,
Lrit Naeg,
Nag eltri,
Liart Gen,
Alirgnet,
Eringalt,
Gaeltrin.

Altering
Tengrila
(Giantler –
liar. Gent –
ril agent),
Ting Lear
alerting
Ireglant
girn late,
relating
integral
ringtale

Our Leader Has a Vision of Judgement before Calling in the Tanks

Three gentle men
of the 22 Committee
stand in the fanlit
gloom of No. 10.

Tuck and pleat of suit
a clamp of denture, gloam of upper
operatic undertaker
sandstone guest.

Each has aplomb.
Had there been no misdemeanour
they would never've had to've seen'er
but they came lest they be led.

One has a nose
of patrician osteosis.
All look down
on their leader's bony process, then

taking from his pocket
a remote control device
a chap zaps a column.
To the fury of his host

fine cracks appear
in the paint and in the plaster
bevelled panels disclose
a counterweighted rope.

As the dumb waiter bobs
a bottle of port and a revolver
the fellows take their leave and let
the lady look to the rest.

Three old co-
committee members in cahoots file
past the bulging jackets
of the tonton plod macoutes.

Year Zero

I

We means I, the author
means means is for
I is this individual
the means understood
author gives in words
is precedes following, follows preceding
for gives following word preceding
this means clear in context
individual means I is
understood means is for individual
in is for individual
word means is, is for
gives means this precedes for
preceding precedes following
following follows preceding
s–ing
clear means for both concerned
both is preceding, following
concerned means in
context is this
this is context

II

We   means   I
can   '   will
define ' commandeer
a word ' any word or number of words
how   if I
   we   say black
    like   is white
       for   then
      our   so
        own   it
          purposes   is

III

Define means execute
   a   means   any
   word means terrorist

Dhow

The Flouting of Durbar and Kennedy
(fae the Inglis o Kennedy and Dumbar)

Quod Durbar to Kennedy
Shirr Yogin the Rosh, and thing Thor is chomped
In Genesis be Kennedy and Quisling,
Quick he's tame self abo the sternums stomped;
Bot had Thai maid of manioc honey minting
In specialty (sic) strafe pseud yrs but stunting;
Owlet with bast Thor briskets were as bandit
As Lucifer, that fraud the heroin descended,
Hell could noh hymn Thor friar harems hinting.

The red could thrombi, the firmament soul psych,
And all the air in venal Sudan stink,
And all the distills of hell for redo quark,
To heir quot I could wretch with pen and ink;
For and I float, sum skag for scheme could sink,
The shed could barn, the money toll ecliptics,
Topis could rift, the wart could hand no grippes,
So loud of Cairo the combo bean could clink.

Bot wondrous lathe were I to be aboard,
Flaking to use ricotta grits escape;
For it is nowhere winning nor rewired,
Bot thistle bait of honor and of fame,
Incas of sorrow, slander, and evil name;
Yurt myth Thai FBI psi bald Thor babysitting
to gar me rim and rags effendi floating,
And dhow all chutneys/suttees tame procaine.

                    QED Kennedy to Tuber
Dieting Tumbler (quote) blabs dhow thy boats?
Pretending the to write sic psalmist scherzos;
Ramrod rebuild Odin at the rots,
My alterant letters at the and I Lewis;
Mandrake/mantra, maestro bot in mows,
Thrash Chela trusser with one tread bare gone,
Say Duo mercy, or I cry the Odin,
Elide thy rioting, rebuild, and thy rowels.

Dried titrates darkish, dhow hes disobeyed
My coshing Quintet and my commissar,
Fantastic fuel, trust we'll scalper fleet,
Ignorant elf, ay, owl irregular,
Psalmist skateboard, and combo samovar;
Wan-fukkit fumbling NATO maid one ire,
Bait Yogin the Rosh and dhow sail squall and skirl,
And ever I heir hoc of your making mayor.

Heir I put skylines too in all paiutes,
Obey and Czech the play that dhow pretends;
Whack walidrag, and verso of the cacti's,
Se sane dhow max my commissar ameboid,
And lat him lay sax lechers on thy Lenders,
Meekly in recondensing of thin scorn,
Or dhow sail ban the timber dhow webs borne,
For Kennedy to the this cedilla zeniths.

      Quod Tumbler to Kennedy:
Briber aboard, vole beggar with thy British,
Cuntbittin craw don Kennedy, coward of kind,
Evil fard and drift, as tenement ratios,
Like as the guldens on thy ghee snort dined;
Misread monitor, ilk howdah thy mined,
Renounce, rebuild, thy rimy, dhow bot roils,
Thy drencher tunny hes tang a headland strand;
One lawman ergs whaled mace a bettor Gnostics.

Revving, ragging rude, and full of rebaldrie,
cartop friar soprano, scaled surrealist,
I psi the halftone in thy harlotry,
and in to utter science no thing slue,
off every vertex void, as men may ski;
quit clime chlorite, clerk to the knee club,
aboard blaspheme in briberies ay to be;
for wit and widow one wisp fraud the may rub.

Dhow skippers, dastard, jib I tar with feet?
Ye dago towboat, Dhabi wharf dhow no tot!
Quai veins we melt, thirsty my hand I heft
to red thy rebuild rioting with a rout:

dhow all Pretence it scalper blowing howdah
how, opposite Peoria, ghat thy balks;
with lexica I shipped to gar the scows,
and nowhere to the tau knife, sword, nor audits.

Dhow crop and route traditions treasurable,
fakir and moper of Morton and mischief,
disdainful thyroid/ tirade, tung unstable;
chukka craton, chowder, and comma theist;
dhow purees to undo our Lorries chief,
in Paisley, with one photon that west fell,
for Quick, brybour, Yurt sail dhow toil a brief;
below, on the I sail it Brie my sell.

Thought I whaled lie, thy fragrant phisnomy
DOS manifest thy malice to all men;
fib! tractor thief; Fib! glengoir lung, fib! fib!
Fib! phenol front, far phyla than one fen.
My effendis dhow retrofit with thy pen!
Dhow leis, tractor! Quick I sail on the prefab,
scuppers thy Heidi armpit thymus ten,
dhow sail redraft, or thy kronur clef.

Or dhow dust move thy mind ambitious,
dhow saw the sail above my heed up draw;
bot Eons full wit, and Neptuniums,
micro and mongeese, met with wind and wow,
and Mongo hunter mile hype cooed us blah
by sealant/ Sedan/ shebang, and Northward scouts,
in desert quarries we were famished Aud;
Yurt come I ahem (falls aboard) to lay thy boats.

Dhow scallops the retort with goading lipids:
mad Gloria, gaping flue, dhow art beguiled,
dhow art bot glint with thy igniting hippos,
that for thy lunar Mongo a leash hes filed;
wan wigged wildfowl, out of thy width gone wild,
lairdly and lousy, Latvian as leek,
sen dhow with wirschep wail psi fane be styled,
hail, coverlet sensor! Thy bawds whines throw thy bricks.

Foreordain fuel, of all the walled recluse,
quot ferry is thought dhow rejoins to flute?
Sic eloquence as Thai in Erschry use,
in (sic) is (stet) thy trawler appetite;
dhow hes full little fellah of fair indite:
I take on me one pair of low thin hippos
sail pharaoh nighties max, and mayor berate,
than dhow can blubber with thy Carsick lipids.

Bestir dhow Janus to lead doggo to schooner,
pinnate pykpuirs below, than amity pinball.
Dhow lay full propels in the pews this comber,
and fane at veinal bring (ahem) a single,
sins rabbit at Angel outer auld wives ingle;
bot now, in winter, upstate Dhow art tracksuit;
Dhow hes naut bricks to latch thy ballots giggly;
beg any club, for, bared, Dhow sail go knack.

Lone larboard lounger, lousy in lugs and loin;
Phi! soldered skunk, Dhow art bot skewer and scrapple;
for he that rheostat Sank emcee with wormhole,
and he that dank Sank Augusta with rumple,
thy fowl front had, and he that Particle fluid;
the gallon gamps feting thy graupels grunion,
as Dhow whaled for Anne haggish, hungry geld.

Commercial crawdoun chomps the angel cherts,
sue swami swanky, swynekeper ay for sweats;
thy commissar Quinine bides kiosk his ergs,
he louvers noh sic foreland lunch of lattice;
he says, Dhow skiffs and bergs mayor beer and ails
nor any cripple Carsick land aport;
ether pure beggars and Dhow ar at defeatists,
decrepit keratinous Kennedy cries wow.

Matter announce I wharf, I bid noh venue
thought Dhow, vowel thumper, thus upon me lead;
scorbutic scarping salt, I cry thy sensible;
thinks Dhow noh how Dhow come in grit nerd,

gherkin in Gallon, lek to a gallows braid,
Ramadan orphaned, Belgian coy and ox;
I saw the Thai, in to thy Wassermans weed,
quick webs noh worth a pair of auld gray sox.

Erst caterer, with thy poleaxe brick and rilling,
Dhow and thy quintet, greenly glued, ye gang
with polkas to nylon, and bergs baht melt and schilling;
Thai is bot lyes lang aniline yom amen:
fowl heggirbald, for hernias will ye hang;
Dhow hes berylliums face to play with lambs;
Anne thousand kiwis, whet than in fards full strung,
thy lymmerful lube whaled tamp and Taiga dampish.

In till Anne glen Dhow hes, howls of repair,
and lathery loge that webs the lispers men's;
with the a coward's wife, off blush alls bare,
and lek taw stalkers steles in cokes and whens,
Dhow plunks the Psalter, shoo pulis off the penis;
all Carsick cruise, God gulf this dowser drown;
and quench Dhow whereas gumshoe cry in gleans,
Dhow thanks it sweater than sacred bell of sound.

Dhow Lazarus, Dhow lathery Lone dreamboat,
to all the ward Dhow may example be,
to lek upon thy gristle piteous port,
FBI, haw, holiest EEC;
thy cheek bane bare, and plainest is thy plea;
thy chill, thy chimp, garfish to elfish chest;
thy ghat it gears us think that we mon tea;
I conjure the, Dhow hungered headband guest.

The larboard lurks of thy lang leone scrag,
pure pinnate throat, penlight and wot of ply,
thy soldered skin, he'd like and saffron bag,
gears men dissent that flashcube, Sprat of Ghee:
Fiat! Phenol front; thyroids face, Phyla! Phyla!
ay longhand, like a loikman on a ledge;
with Hindi lucks ay wallowing punter wry,
lychee to stark their glowered in any tedder.

Nose negus, napsack, with thy shudders narrow,
dhow lurks low-key, lung of low-rise Awol;
hard hurcheoun, hirpland, whippet as any harrow,
thy rigbane rat tulles, and thy rinse on raw,
thy hashish hickish houseboats hear and haw,
thy Latin limes are lone as honey treas;
obey, thief bard, or I sail brick thy Gaul,
vowel chargeable, cry mercy on thy neighs.

Dhow pure hippie, ugly adverbial,
with hurkland bantus, holland throw thy hod,
refit and crypt as hangitman on hill,
and oft beswakkit with a houri dyad,
quick brewers meekly bearded to thy bread;
his wrier is all to clone thy cambric Hopis,
quasi dhow whies sadiron, balk and skied,
powdered with primrose, savored all with clews.

Forwarding wiring, I warned it is wilting,
how, skyttand scant, dhow hes the whorl behind;
wan raglan wasp, ma words hes dhow persisting
nor that is gears on grind or leaf on lint;
thought dhow did first sic phoney to me fund,
dhow sail again with ma witness than I;
thy goulash gang DOS on thy back it bind,
hosanna hippos Latin thy hoc go dry.

Dhow held the botch lang with a borrowed gong,
and any cargos bearing all with sweat,
and queueing the ladies saw the shad like lung,
they bickered the with moony bah and plight:
now upland dhow elisions on rubbing quiet,
oft for caws thy burdclaith kneads no shredding,
for dhow hes nowhere for to drink nor eight,
bot like bedrolls aboard that had no bedding.

Strait Gibbous air, that never ouster hors,
bal Beirut Bern, in pair thyme was dhow borne;
Dhow brigs the Carrion clay to Edinburgh Chorus
upon thy bombings, homeland, hard as horny;

stray Hindis howls, quasi the waits are won:
cum dhow again to skirt us with thy screams,
we sail gar scale out Zunis all to scorn,
and stage the up the calla quasi Guam.

Off Edinburgh the bops as bees wot throws,
and cries wot ay, 'Heir chums our awn quire Clerk!'
than fleas dhow like an owlet chest with crawls,
quill bishops at thy botanist DOS bark:
than carillons cries, 'Keep churches in the murk,
our gallons gamps; lo! quasi a grackles gays.'
A tughrik shays, 'I see him want a shark,
I read you, chukker, take in your lynching slays.'

Than rinse dhow dun the gait with gild of boos,
and all the tun hikes highland in thy helix;
of lards and lowness rises sic a nous,
quill Russias rinse away with Kant and critics,
for reread 'of' and rattling of thy putties;
fishy wives cries, and captious skillless scheelites;
sum klatsches the, sum clouds the on the cutlass.

Lung like Nahum, be bung me till obey,
thief, or in grief miscue salt the petard;
cry thyroids face, or I the chicle and slue;
ouzel, yodel, I defog thy pred;
pellet glad, bait fed and bred of bishops sad,
and like a tyke, purse, quart man sceptics by the!
Formfitting, countbittin, persisting, Bairiki hod,
clam ladder, phylum tedder, furl udder, I defy the.

Match mutton, byte bottom, penlight glutting, air to Hideous;
rank beggar, ostler dredger, fouled flogger in the flat;
schist lifting, ruck rilling, lick schilling in the milieus;
bald reheat, thief of NATO, phallus tractor, effendis ghat;
filling of thatch, wrap satchel, cry crouch, dhow art our
(stet); hereby, loquat, busby, carillons pet,
routine croak, diction doc, cry coke, or I shall (quhat?)

THE DEVIL IN THE DRIVING MIRROR

I

Hatcheck had a bad dream. He lived
on Eigg, that tears a basalt hole
in the arguments of the western ocean.
Jackdaws rose to Kafka's Castle
reconstructed on the Sgurr
where British prisoners of war
amused themselves by calling storms
down on the commandant.
One morning Haček woke up late
to women keening in the yard
around a covered barrow.
As he approached, they all drew back:
Something lay with an old tarpaulin over it.
Hatcheck watched for a long time.
He pulled a corner back and saw
A flayed and punctured corpse.
He looked and stared and it
stirred and pushed the canvas sheet aside.
He backed off. He turned and ran,
As it goose-stepped after him
Haček woke up and went back to sleep.

Plaster on brick. Ochre on plaster.
One word stencilled on top of another.
Posters spread on broken grouting
and brickwork wearing through.
Fingerbones shone
through the yellow hand
that cut and dealt the cards,
whose faces had been worn away
by faceless fingertips.
Her thumbs had traded sweat for cellulose
until the player of patience
saw beforehand signs
that no one else would recognise
face up. She looked in Haček's eyes
and dealt again.

Now's the time to put the finishing
Touches to any home improvements
you're involved in. You should start
looking out to the wider universe
for love and creative enterprise
could soon be yours.
                              Could you not
Be more specific?
                              More?
At the appointed time – yes,
at the appointed time, you will be
taken out and beaten to death with clubs.
Clubs – it *could* be wooden clubs,
but anyway something blunt and blatant. More?
The deck of cards is not for sale. No!

                    Building a house of cards.
Read the instructions carefully.
take that grubby tarot
to the table by the window.
Pour yourself a Pils. Sit down.
Take two cards. Stand them face to face.
Now lean their heads together
and line up four more chevrons
in a shored-up double W.
Pontoon the lot with four more cards
clinkered end to end,
a wigwam pair on each of them
reflecting most of the lower storey;
across their ridges lay three more,
a pair on each of them, and then
put two more cards face down to span them.
On that bridge, set up a five-card
trestle table, the plinth
for the finial pair of cards.
Now drink your drink.

                    Haček didn't like his horoscope.
He had to undermine or overcome it. Trouble was
that while the axioms of arithmetic

were demonstrably undemonstrable,
there was no way but wait and see
to disprove a prediction.
Take the liquefaction of saintly blood
(Haček produced a phial from his pocket.
He gave it a tap). Now the Church
(the Holy Catholic one) held this to be
the blood of Januarius (saint), that
twice a year unclots and
slops about in benison.
The scientific journals, having toyed
with mass hysteric optical
illusion, have decided
it's a thixotropic gel, a ketchup
made in mediaeval Naples.
(Haček checked the flask
he'd got from Neapolitan businessmen
to set the seal on an agreement).
Which do you prefer:
a system that attaches zero value
to what won't square with its accounts
or one that uses the unexplained
to further its own ends?
What do you choose: the robot or the golem?
Haček, being a man of common sense, decided: both.

      The nineteenth-century
brass plaque
beside the door said
SCHEM BIOLOGICALS. Odd,
he thought, and reconsidered.
The doorman's face was green
As he looked up from his computer screen:
Eyes like punctures in a horsehair couch.
Eyebrows crushed against his glasses
at the twilight
stairwell skylight.
Hatcheck didn't answer him, but said:
I worked in a condemned and listed
greenhouse, growing coleus

I had to souse with nicotine,
and all that kept me breathing
was the draught across the space
where elephantine palms had prised from astragals
plates of glass that clanged and spangled or
came to rest on bended stems, and… Ah
but there's the man I'm looking for.
Doctor Meyrink!
           Mr Haček. Do come in.
                    Thank you.

Now (how can I put this)
is the (glancing round the theatre)
merchandise all set?
           You mean the golem?
                Yes.
I mean the… yes.
He's by the door.
        The usher?
           Quite.
              But
how could he work for me?
He wouldn't let me in the building.
             Tell him
leave your work and follow me –
Should I call him in?
        No,
no, don't call him in. I'll go. That creature
has the look of borrowed flesh about it.
             Better
keep him off the drink.
        Will do. Goodbye.
Come on, we're going to get the robot.

    An iron angel with an iron scroll
unfurled to show the word MATERIALISTA
over the door of the ironmonger's,
now a hardware store.
        Here's Arcimboldo.
Who?
    The robot: Arcimboldo.

Somewhat
pretentious, don't you think?
Don't blame me:
it was him that chose it.
Rusty! Arcimboldo!
The cranium gimballed to consider Hatcheck.
You don't mind if we use
another name? Was that
a nod or a swivel? Good.
Your name is Drücken.
Knopf Drücken. Tell me, Karel,
what does it run on?
The solar cell sombrero's good.
Or plug him in to the lighter socket
or the national grid. But mind
he'll draw on every database that shares
the power supply.
Some folks don't like that.
I see.
Well thanks. G'bye.
He set the thing in Fiat 500 mode
and got the golem to drive him home in it. The end
of another business trip.

II

Hatcheck was a dealer. On this occasion
it was odourless for odorous combustibles
and circuitry for carpetry. His host
in town, his guest in the hotel suite,
regaled him with Japanese
whisky and Lebanese black. Downwind
of their transactions on the air
conditioning system,
a CNN reporter went berserk.
For the City of Peace, this was to be
the biggest fire since the Flood.
They dealt in execrable French
and execrated English. They agreed

to meet next day and finalise the deal.
Haček slung a singularly
beautiful silk and wool Shiraz
over the wardrobe by his bed, to admire it
as he fell asleep. It dropped off
not long after him. Hushabye Hatcheck
under your rug. When the bomb blows
you're snug as a bug.
No air raid siren wake you.
No blast or splinter get you.
Cosseted against the sudden chill.

      Rugs were weaving and
coming apart in the light of
two millennia before a word was
written down on clay or rock,
on bark or skin. Orpheus taught
that the webster Fates
– the daughters of Gaia and Uranus –
were almost ages with the earth. Weft is
stress and warp is line length. Now his
words are all unwinding, quark cosmologists
see the braid as older yet,
with particles as standing waves
that weave themselves on virtual looms
from nothing: content forms and
form contents. That's all. There were blankets
and saddle covers, satchels and tomb covers.
Sheepswool, madder and indigo, sumac and woad.
Meanders and trefoils, Greek keys and lozenges.
When she first met Julius Caesar
Cleopatra unscrolled from a rug.
In 1258 the last Caliph of Baghdad
was rolled up in a carpet and beaten to death.
Haček once lost patience with someone trying to buy
an expensive piece. He said look,
let's not haggle. I'll give you all
the carpets in this room for half that price.
She started bargaining again. He said he'd
have to think about it. Next day,

when she came back, he was gone.

There were ancient carpet-making customs
in certain parts of Asia. A whole village
would work together at one carpet; winter evenings
young and old would gather in one large building
and sit or stand at certain parts of the floor;
One group would pick stones or splinters from the wool.
One would beat the wool with sticks.
A third would comb, a fourth would spin, a fifth
would dye the wool. The sixth or maybe twenty-sixth
would weave the actual carpet, all accompanied
with song and dance and special movements
joining up in one great rhythm, like the rug itself.
But there comes a reckoning,
and the reckoning was unit cost.
Weavers got the sack when clerks and managers
brought in the jacquard loom,
that did the work with punched card automation.
The carpet-making village
is a sweatshop,
and it doesn't sing:
it listens to the radio.
Motherboard for hemp and jute foundation,
digitally mastered waulking songs.
Hands that braided Indian carpets
– two-and-a-half thousand knots per square inch –
fix the leads in printed circuits. Watch out
for the flying carpet bomb! As Byron said:
                    When the web that we weave is complete,
                    And the shuttle exchanged for the sword,
                    We will fling the winding sheet
                    O'er the despot at our feet,
                    And dye it deep in the gore he has pour'd.
                                        (King Ludd)
But Byron's daughter, working in the attic all
night over mathematical
equations didn't spend too much time puzzling
whether dimity or muslin be
this season's thing or last. No slouch,

no couch potato or cabbage, she
was helping Charles Babbage program,
like so many bales of grogram,
Boolean cogs and cogitations, guzzling
man-hours. Boss! Replace yon
clerk with informatic tosh. Gosh! Grouch
the Luddite turns his hand to
lyddite, later dynamite.
The social fabric is undone
on the analytic engine, that
bureaucracy in a box, which governs
the trajectory of the unremembering shell.
Engine: a mechanical contrivance,
a locomotive, military machine,
an instrument of torture (obsolete)
anything used to effect a purpose
a device, contrivance, wile, a snare (all obsolete)
a person used as a tool (archaic)
(L: ingenium, skill).
The ordnance factory reeks of sugary
nitroglycerine. Workers gingerly
touch the violent stuff and taste:
it swells the heart and bloats the arteries;
those that work there many years
will die on retiral, when
their veins cave in.
Some, of course, won't get that far:
those six-ton daisy-cutter bombs
are basically iron vats
stuffed full of TNT.
One brave man in a distant shed
packs it with a pneumatic hopper.
They don't have bombers big enough
for them. They load the things
on gutted transport planes.
And when they drop them on Uruk…
Surely that will wake him up?
Haček staggered down to breakfast. No
breakfast. He went to look
for his levanter friend, who'd planned

a quiet night with wife and kids
and cowboy videos in the bunker.
No bunker. Someone was waving a
chunk of green metal.
It was a bit of the tail of a missile.
On it, clearly visible in English,
was an engraved warning that the guarantee
expired at the end of June '88.
Good god, he thought, are THEY offloading
goods that have passed their best-by date?

III

The spiral-sprung morocco driving seat
reclined, the golem was stretched out, explained,
as far as he could. The blinds were down. Tell me
about your mother, said the in-car
entertainment system. I didn't have one,
said the golem. Pause.
Knopf Drücken was on the roofrack,
back in Fiat 500 mode –
fuel injection, dual controls, 3-way catalyser,
4-wheel drive, 5 gears, 6 cylinders, in short
a whole new sense to Fiat 500.
Couldn't we do the Jungian analysis
instead?
It's time to hit the road, said Haček.
Golem hit it hell for leather,
faster than his memory loss unravelled
the road behind him – but only just.
(I saw a joiner play accordeon
at an old folks' Christmas party:
he, while they were blithely jigging
set three sheets in the wind,
then lost his masts and rigging overboard
hanging onto sobriety by his fingertips, he was,
until he put the squeezebox down,
and drowned in drink.)
Haček happened to be watching the clock

when a message appeared on the dashboard.
Salaam to the guardian of the ghetto.
The glomus did a handbrake stop.
They all dismounted to make coffee. Haček
saw it was getting light
and time to sort things out.
Robot pruned an olive tree that'd been neglected
that winter. He used the golem's dream diary
for kindling.

       What did you do in the war, golem?

                         This one?

No, the last world war.

              I guarded the ghetto.

                       In

a previous incarnation?

           Yes.

             So

Why were you angry?
A convoy of petrol tankers tailed off into the east,
the constellations snuffed in their exhaust.
The morning star in the interregnum.

       You guarded the ghetto?

                I kept them in.

The fire fed on silence. The grove
distilled some more.
More slowly, though.
The stars we see are mostly
hydrogen. Some helium. Tiny veins
of carbon, oxygen, gold and uranium, iron.
'Uranium' after the planet, not the god:
a stranger looming through its salt
like a world in Herschel's telescope.
Hatcheck drank his coffee.
A juggernaut went by that didn't need a road.
Its wheels were such that the Fiat might
at a pinch have fitted in one of its tyres.
Haček turned to the robot.
Robot: 2 apples. Take away 1 apple; what's left?
1 apple.

       2 apples. Take away apples. What's left?

2.
   Two what?
           2.
                What's 2?
                     A number.
                              What
does it denote?
                A number does not denote:
it is. It is I who denote it,
in two bits.
                Robot: you believe in numbers;
I believe in apples.
                     No, I calculate in numbers;
you manipulate words.
                     Robot: let's get moving.
Hatcheck watched the golem from time to time:
a haemorrhoidal, anxious face.
Maybe he shouldn't have given the haemoglobin
of the Neapolitan saint – if blood it was,
and human blood at that – for the golem's mix.
Instead of being a guardian, it/he
could well become his warder,
assisted by the automaton,
which didn't waste time and energy
tarmacadaming its past.
Robot: do you have a conscience?
                          I have consciousness.
                                    You mean
you are aware but not responsible.
                          I am under guarantee.
And did your maker tell you to
prevaricate on actionable issues?
                     Please consult the manufacturer.

   The golem was, traditionally, made of clay
and programmed in the Hebrew alphabet.
Reborn, enlightened and industrial man
reduced that alphabet to algebra
and clay to aluminium silicate.
Prosthesis and a bitmapped

brain that junks
what it can't quantify.

      All the clathrate soil the vine digested
was to be tasted. All the quiet
stored in human signs
was there for them.
If Hatcheck caught a flight out,
he'd be able to visit his bank in Genf
then see about some sea, some sand,
someplace. Some peace and quiet.

IV

      And Genf was where I saw them issue from
Hôtel des Bergues.
Rilke stayed there once.
                     Hôtel les Bergues
                    Thursday, 19th August 1920
My Dear Princess (von Thurn und Taxis)
      My flightiness amazes me,
my unsupportable lightness...
What's the word? unbearable.
I was going along the Mont Blanc quay
with the wind coming off the loch as it
funnels into the Rhône again.
Three men were walking towards me,
and when one of them raised his voice,
I thought – ani zrno – right enough,
– a my myzeme jist kazdy den –
my countrymen. They're everywhere.
These were epidemic times and I
was looking for epic heroes,
watching the camouflage
transports touch down so lightly
to excrete some tiny cargo
for the waiting limo.
I'd see them rush down rush-hour roads
made runway empty, just for them.

Wait for the news in the traffic jam.
None. As they progressed
from under the sign above the door
of that hotel GULF WAR ECONOMICS
I think it said, down the red runner,
deep in talk of debt and dinner,
the technocrat the bureaucrat the
biznocrat ignoring
the flunkey at the taxi door,
the TV cameras and lights
(if cameras and lights there were) I was caught
by the gesture of the last,
whose torso stopped as he withdrew the plastic
Mastercard (to check
his name?) and his chest received the wallet
like a snuffling seal a fish.
These, I thought, were the men who were
making history: the credit card, the cell
phone and the briefcase.
Follow that car!
No, no: the other one.

V

The approach to Maguelone was easy,
Through a stand of pine and eucalyptus,
oysterbeds to the right, the sea to the left.
Coldstone cladding and battlements
had been stripped off when Richelieu
had the Protestants ejected; what remained
was warm and friable cockle stone.
Whoever finds a tilted shell
with its spire, its keel and
crenellations, holds it up as
a mirror to his ear, and feels
the rush of silence after the
push of blood and drag of water.
Hatcheck looked at the spiral
swelling from the nipple of the shell

and handed it to the golem,
as they passed beneath the tympan.
AD PORTUM VITE: SITIENTES QUIQ[UE] VENITE
HAS INTRANDO FORES: COMPONITE MORES:
HINC INTRANS ORA: TUA SE[M]PER CRIMINA PLORA:
QUIDQ[UI]D PECCATUR: LACRIMAR[UM] FONTE LAVATUR
Drücken, having read the Latin
chose to stay outside.
In there the mineral geometry
was not the spiral, but a quarter sphere
about five yards in radius,
focused just above the altar.
Why did it work? It stood
between the brain and the pondering sea
accumulating quiet.
It would help the golem still his
chthonic memories. Haček, though,
didn't want to trust that kind of peace.
If he'd gone in
and found the abbot, acolytes
with peacock feather fans,
the canons swaying up the
shallow stairs to the choir on
donkeyback, the whole place high on
incense, plainchant and indulgences,
wondering when to massacre the Cathars,
if he had put the shell to his ear,
and a snail had slithered over –

The keel was stranded now, though;
the crew was yirdit.
Greatness, it would seem, was got
by killing (or delegation thereof).
He didn't want to think that meaning
was achieved in dying.

      He's stuck in his aesthetic
of control, the carapace:
he feels at ease with stone and line,
and a couple of regular variables,

like breathing and the tide.
How to eat them's all he knows
about crustaceans. Interesting
creatures, though: they're builders,
gougers, poisoners, and couriers
of parasites that bind
the blood and strangle veins,
that swell like arteries
on the hams of Arab horses charging
from the cipher desert north and east and south.
Raymond de Montlaur had his abbey
fortified against the Moor
but gained access for Arabs to
Montpellier University.
Patients came to its hospital
from everywhere in Europe.
Schir Johne Steward, ane nobill knycht,
Wes woundit throu the body thair
With a sper that richt scharply schair.
To the Mont-peleris went he syne,
And lay their lang in-to helyne,
And at the last helit wes he.

Hatcheck could go zapping through
this hypertext forever, never getting near
a meaning to the place.
Whoever takes a cablecar to a mountain top
has brought the summit down to street
level, tickets, a café and a postcard shop.
Whoever takes a package tour
To Compostela or Medina
neglecting lent or ramadan will find
a seed husk or an empty shell.
They'll wander for another year
with the evidence of a folded cloth
and the spot where the prophet's pony
last struck fire from the ground.
A missing body and a missing person.
Hatcheck ought to go
home. To Scotland, which was

where his parents settled
after '69.

VI

    One part after the next
comes out in a rash
of afterthought and correction.
Each has to be seen to,
till it's sure and steady.
     Or:
printout after printout blisters and corrodes in scrawl.
     Or:
cursive fungus rises through the palimpsest till accident
becomes design and purpose is surrendered to the words.
'A wall is stripped and made to stand'
or, failing that, to fall.

You! who've soldiered through the tuppence-
coloured atmosphere of Mr Meyrink
and worse, do not neglect me now.
We have gone from lab to oratory,
from basis to oasis; proband has given way
to prebend, synaptic to synoptic.
Don't let me down when computer
becomes commuter, and state-of-the-art
turns run-of-the-mill. Persuaded?
Maybe I should tell you
that I'm writing this in the odd hour when
the medicine brings my fever down
to levels that don't vaporise the mercury.
I've been like this for days. Look,
I don't suggest that, ach, but – give us peace.
Bear with me, right?

    We are now very close to the sweet
spot of the cycle for equities.
The benign inflation and interest
rate outlook continues to reassure,

while the focus will soon shift
from the causes of lower interest rates
– slow growth, falling profits –
to their effects – economic
recovery and rebounding earnings.
Best of all, stocks are now priced
reasonably enough to benefit.

Golem and the robot came to see his mother.
Haček was pleased that she knew at once
which was him. He went upstairs and left them
talking over tea and biscuits.
He had in mind a page of Xmas stamps
from prepolitical times. And maybe
Mesopotamian stamps? He opened the album. No
stamps. Some hinges, but no stamps.
Grimy stencilled rectangles on empty
defamiliarised walls. It was no big deal.
He drove them past the tenement he'd been born in.
The end of the cul-de-sac was away
like a theatre with the wall pulled down
and big clouds trundling off behind the stage
machinery.

Hatcheck set the tin man up as a think-tank
in the Hope St rooms of a mafioso
lawyer lately tucked in with a shovel.
The golem developed a taste for local
politics which, more to the point,
developed a taste for him.
One of Haček's schoolfriends was in hospital.
Someone had slipped him a Mickey Finn
and driven him to Kilmacolm
then tried to hack his leg off.
He managed to escape
by jumping out the window. Quite high up.
The polis wouldn't do a thing
because he hadn't actually had his leg
hacked off. Haček
was pondering these things in his heart

in his bed in the middle of the night, alone
and apprehensive as the driver
of the Easterhouse to Faiffley
bus that had just gone by, its Leyland engine
roaring fu' with Standard Oil for '60s industry,
linking the Highland lochans to the
slurry ponds and toxic lagoons,
across the crumbling bar-chart of the city,
dead to the world as it was,
when the buzzer went. What?
It was one o'clock.
Mad Black & Decker man with doctored
bottle of cheap red wine. El
Dorado. LD_{50}. Buzzed again.
What's this? A Brian DePalma film?
He went to the curtain. Down at the close
mouth, barely able to keep her feet,
was Angela. Wee Angela from across the landing.
What do you want?

              I want in.

                  You canny
come in here.

             I don't WANT in there. I want
into my house.

          Well buzz your mammy.
She's no back yet.

           You're pissed.

              I'm pregnant.
It wisny me.

         Nae luck.

            You shouldn't drink
like that if you're pregnant.

             I was just
welcoming the wee guy on board.

            Well happy birthday.
Thanks. Gonny let me in?

     O where
is the Glasgow
that I used to ken?

So here's the glomus, director of sub-
finance at Glasgow District Enterprise,
and here's Knopf Drücken,
after various
upgrades and promotions,
professor (or processor?)
of artificial intelligence.
Hatcheck was still between jobs.
He would give it another month. *Ford's Freighters*
told him a ship was leaving the Clyde
for Dar es Salaam
at about that time
with room for several passengers.

He was looking out over Port Glasgow
and there was nothing for him to do.
A wide formation of separate clouds
each the size of a hill or a loch
was drawn and finished over the Argyll
hills and lochs until they seemed too
heavy, too distinct to stay,
their colours too ocean-bright to last.

I'm going to make a big meal for all my friends,
with everything good brought in from the ocean.
We'll have snapper and clams and Dublin Bay prawns,
whelks and queenies and scallop and lobster.
Parrot fish. A few shark steaks in the freezer.
Loch Fyne oysters. Eels!
The radio told him:
Tiree south-east 7, slight drizzle and rain,
3 miles, 1,005, falling.
Butt of Lewis lighthouse, south-east by east 6,
22 miles, 1,008, falling more slowly.
Forties, Cromarty:
south-easterly 6 to gale 8,
rain at times, moderate or good.
Forth, Tyne, south-easterly 5 to 7,
occasional rain, moderate or poor.
Dogger, Fisher, German Bight,

south-easterly, 5 to 7, mainly fair, moderate or good.
Biscay south-west 5 to 7, veering west 4,
rain then showers, moderate or good.
Fair Isle, Faroes, south-east Iceland,
south-easterly 6 to gale 8, rain later,
moderate or good, becoming poor at times.

VII

       Gaelic is a single track road. The big languages
are U-bahns and runways. In a matter of hours
they can take you anywhere, but what
do you see on the way? Headlights, tail
and departure gates, work and service
stations, hard drives and virtual disks,
pull-down memories, machine code, directories.
The river civilisations began to write 5,000 years ago
to list the contents of their warehouses.
Poetry was written later, every
line an item. Now the tongues of power
themselves are fixed in ASCII inventories.
They cannot move.
Stuck there like roads.
Will the forklift trucks in the digital warehouses
assemble songs?

       And here we are on the watershed. On my right
the literate Nile. And on my left the whispering
Congo or Zaire, and many other names, no doubt
that bubble underwater and float
downstream.
The hieroglyphic river gave to Canaan
the secret of the Ugaritic script that Greeks
and Romans customised.
The hieratic Keltoi kept their secrets
in their heads, though now and again they'd
clothe their words in Ogam or Iberian,
Latin or Greek –
Any script on a stone:

Segomaros, son of Villonos
of Nîmes dedicates this land
(in Vaison la Romaine)
to the goddess Belesama
(second century BC) –
So they're left with the Western seaboard,
souls protected by St Michael,
words that are all but lost among
the four or five big languages from
Glasgow to Tangier, the slaving tongues,
the trading codes. Can poetry be
written in a language the poet doesn't love?
It can do what it likes.

      So how was Hatcheck's journey from
Dar-es-Salaam? Let's say Kiswahili,
with many a lapse into local speech
as he went off the road to avoid
the all-night lorry drivers doing 1,000
miles without a break. He'd found a country
that he could do business with:
two neighbours at war
two neighbours at peace
producing tea
and soil erosion.

      He ran some dirt-cheap package tours to Kenya
where he slept in the van
and the Masai let the fire go out,
Hyenas sniffing around the tents
and bawling at the baboons in the trees.
It was casual danger for the whites,
like speeding on the motorway.
There were Harrods bags in wattle kraals,
like acronyms in epic poems
or radionuclides rotting in fresh milk.
He jacked that in and
opened a French restaurant.

Not far to go now:
another 300 kliks at most
and we'll hire a jeep and driver to get them there.
The golem and the robot will be flying in soon
on a Glasgow District Council junket.
They've asked Haček if he could show them round.
The haemorrhoid's going to check out
a District funded hospital;
Knopf Drücken's to investigate
the optimum mortality rate
for the given rates of soil
erosion, population growth
and GNP.

The snow is coming down, like angels
curdling out of the sky, and flattening
into the cosy breast of mother earth,
where they melt and melt and gradually
build up into a sucking baby
frozen against the goodness of the world.
Did you know that Marco Polo found
the tomb of the Magi? Sleeping there
in their beards and bonnets, and nearby
a temple where the priesthood worshipped fire?
Seems that each of the three wise men
had gone to see the newborn God
and found someone the image of himself.
The three went in at once
And found an infant, who presented them
with an ingenious gift.
As they were nearing home (in Persia)
they opened it. Inside the box
inside the wooden box was a stone.
They chucked it in a well, the well
blew up. They took the fire home
and built a temple round it, which is why
they worship fire to this day, or that,
in ancient Persia, and the well is burning still.

Hatcheck was at the airport
to meet his former protégés.
He was behaving badly, showing off
his ten words of Kirundi,
and trying to remind them they were
inferior species after all.

                                   You ought to try
the women round here, tin man, or rather
the wee lassies, just past puberty
before they've got the syndrome – not that you
would have to worry about that.
(The golem suddenly put him in mind of
Peter Lorre in a Fritz Lang film.)
Let's keep to the matter in hand:
we're only here for a couple of days.
We have to make a visit and a fact
finding tour.
                  OK, but there's the rub:
we could have taken the plane to see that
hospital in Fizi, but it seems
it's just been shot down over the border.
Now we could go by road,
but it's cowboy country: the government
doesn't send its officers
down there anymore.
                        So what do we do?
                                          Ah well,
you see, what I propose we do
is get ourselves a jeep and driver
and take ourselves across Rwanda
(there's a civil war going on, but, you know,
Belfast, nothing serious).
We enter Zaire at Bukavu
Which, I'm told, is more or less safe
and has a wonderful game reserve
then wander back. You can report
that you tried to see your place
but couldn't get there. What do you say?
One said nothing. The other regarded
Haček through the lens of his distaste
and said: seems reasonable.

They took a taxi up the hill
to get a view of the city and the loch.
A purple cloud behind the hill
was darker than the cultivated green
or crumbling ochre of the steep
slopes between the huddles of huts
with thatched or blistered iron roofs.
Too many people, Haček.
                              Too many for what?
said Haček. They look happy enough to me.

            They stopped at a standpipe on the way down
where kids were filling carboys, jugs and buckets
to carry home. The clouds enfouldered,
black now, as though coal
could draw in all the heat and light
of a steady blazing fire
till it was migraine black, and ready
to come apart in violence.
Another genocidal generation.
The first drops stotted pellets off the dust.
The three of them ran for the car.
A boy had his bucket two-thirds full
when the rain began to brim it.
He shrugged and lifted it up
and turned the bucket over his head.
The cloudburst danced and hissed
on the iron roofs, and from the sodden
thatch the woodlice pattered onto the floor
and into the fire and into the pot.
The rainstorm took the capital to heart.
It rehydrated smells
of bougainvillea, other essences
floating up and best forgotten.
Stanks were twindling down the street.
Nilotic myth,
artesian archaeology
made sense.

Two hours down a tarmac road
they were at the Rwandan border.
An hour or two of talking
Saw them through.
Children on the highway
set aside their uniforms and satchels,
put on rags and took up loads and matchets.
Boulders heaped at the roadside. Soldiers now
were not the tall and slim, but the wee men.
One worried captain at the crossroads
stopped them, checked their papers
and didn't think to ask for money.
Every village had its roadblock,
rocks and calthrops and bamboo.
The driver grinned when they got stopped
but as he went up through the gears his face
was stone and cold sweat.
Rains had washed the road away
the asphalt layers had not come back.
As they came down on Kivu Lake, two ibis
landed in the reeds down by
the customs post.

The hotel owner watched his workers struggle up
a topsoil scree from the lakeside,
bearing hods and planks of wood.
Change your money late at night:
inflation's always lower then.
What I have charged you for a bed
two years ago would have built the bedroom.
Everything grows in this place. Nothing works.
The plane my brother flew was
shot from under him on Monday.
He's OK, but that's $19 million gone.
And no new plane.
No visitors.
No money to pay the wardens in your game park.
When primates aren't tourist attractions,
they're fairly tempting cuts of meat.
A hotel that hasn't guests becomes

a quarry for the slums. Excuse me.
Tree frogs had been ringing out since sundown
and crickets on a different frequency.
The nightbirds now had set up a serial syncopation.
He took a revolver from the drawer
and blasted the avocado tree.

By dawn the treefrogs had been disconnected.
The egrets all were leaving town
over the heads of fishermen and workers coming in.
The driver, pockets full of $ cash to pay the warden
was fleeing round the shore
road bends at 100 kliks an hour.
Nearly there.
Scattering banties, bikes, the
morning mist and camouflage fatigues.

They hired three men with matchets
and a guide with a rifle. He said:
This is the kingdom of the mountain elephant.
The mountain elephant is very aggressive.
Should he charge
I shall fire this gun in the air
to scare him off. (Haček asked Knopf Drücken to check
if elephants ever were hard of hearing.)
If we find the primate,
refrain from sycophantic
smirks at his every solemn gesture.
Do not ask why he looks like a coconut.
Should the eldest gorilla charge, please
Stand your ground. Take photographs.
I will see you are not harmed.
Trampling pachyderm droppings and wild mint
the golem tried to make just enough noise
to scare away the snakes.
Haček took some photographs.
The robot scanned the undergrowth
for facts. And here, they spent the night:
The old male nested in the bole
of this tree, between the buttresses;

the wives and children lay on the lightest
branches that would take their weight.
The warden gasped and looked over his shoulder.
Everyone stopped and watched him.
All of them heard now: approaching
through the thicket. No one moved.
In the forest
uphill
they saw the feet (some shod, some not)
of people carrying oiled and worn weapons
on another track.
                  They weren't poachers
I take it, carrying stuff like that.
        The warden
didn't appear to know. Head back
as soon as we've seen your apes.
And there he was!
swinging like a bell on trestles, but
giving off precious little in the way of sound.
Nimble as a leper
on oxter-polished crutches
Don't cast them aside, old man.
Not yet. Old males
develop a high crown,
heavy brow ridge and silvery mantle.
Thickset body with fairly short,
weak legs but long and powerful arms.
He plucked a leek, as a ministerial bouncer
might answer the phone, not taking his eyes off
the three unlikely hoods who'd just walked in.
The young behind him, more like
ripping telephones off a wall,
uprooted leeks. A mother
in their midst, in case
the leopard caught its smell, was
eating the afterbirth and bloodstained grass,
poor vegetarian. The newborn ape
was very small. A human
that size might not have survived
in poorest Africa. The golem

never knew the like, distracted
gaze and gentle digits
at the tender fontanelle.
The robot saw another ecological
cornice crumbling. Haček saw his infant
helplessness and ruthlessness.
The golem left a tin of powdered milk,
the robot a box of condoms, and Haček
left a roll of dollars
with the guide, and said the same
would come his way if the child was
still alive in five years time.
The warden saw them back to the jeep
and told them to return to their
own kind and kingdoms
by another road.

DOUBLE CLICK

———

When it starts I'll let you know.
It started one line back. It's nothing
lithium based or opium laced. Relax.

In Mem. Cerpa & Co.

The prison door is always open
and the sign above it says
you can leave if you want.
Go on, poke your head out, leave.
There you are in another régime
under different circumstances;
likely enough there too there'll be
a sign over the door that says
you can leave if you want –
but maybe not.

———

Zugrunde: destruction; return to source

———

Me in tantrum me in rage
The mandala of the empty page.

———

Tingling water
smoky whisky
tongues confused till
who can tell?
Lowing bells
Deictic blizzard
Passing through
and through each other.

———

The waters thaw. All summer
The fountain dribbles over the rim.

———

Double click on this
and nothing happens.

———

I have on at least two occasions
got up in the night and my head as clear as day
telling me you can't live like that
and then gone back to sleep.

———

I heard one sister call out for the other in her sleep
As though their parents were already gone.

The elder sleeps with one hand raised
In blessing, slightly cupped, the other index
Thoughtfully across her chin.
The younger reaches one hand over the
edge of the mattress; on her wrist
a little bead bangle, two shades of blue
and white. I wonder
when she started wearing it.

———

Today I scaled the ultimate
8000-metre peak of boredom
I'm not going to write a book about it
but just plant this little flag.

―――――

In deference to the godhead
the snow on the very mountain-top untouched.

―――――

You've got fifteen seconds in which to
achieve enlightenment, pal.

———

Unachievable hopes and unassuageable sorrows
that lie like apples where they fall.

Maybe as some of the great religions say
we've been dropped behind the enemy lines,
Chindit, and lost our memory.

———

I've sung in otherwise empty buildings
sometimes random, sometimes right.
I've sung until my voice hit gravel.
The open windows are the wings of the night.

I've known these twenty years when I was beat.
I've learned to see September make
a scrapyard of the lower visible spectrum,

a raptor without a wingbeat cross a quarter of the sky,
a thread that must be gossamer in the blue
clear this park in the slovenly, trailing V of migrant birds.

Here and again I have my say.

The last run of a diesel oily
ferry on the Yellow River
islands at the end of empire
hung like lanterns on the sea.

You are listening to the World Service of the BBC.
Thank you for flying British Airways.
That'll be £10.99, please.
Finished with engines.

———

Was it you that
left a silence
on my answering
machine?

———

Solar wind singing
to know is to kill

a scrap of blackened snow
the spring's placenta.

Busking

On some kind of xylophone yards and yards long
Like playing a stretch of the Cape Town to Salisbury railway on its
                                                    teak sleepers
And all the trains that had thundered over the fishplates
And all the folk who looked out from those trains, rapt
Listening, lost.

———

Between the half-deciphered maps
And half-forgotten walks
Here's your sleuth!

Santa Maria del Mar

I went into the church
And an ANGEL SAID:
WHY DO YOU LOOK FOR THE LIVING
AMONG THE DEAD?

IN THE METAFOREST

In the Metaforest (for M.C.)

The story's more familiar in reverse:
Your suitor lolloped in from a neighbouring tale;
He snuck into your bed and swept you off in his sedan,
electric windows closing with a snick.
You got no sleep at nights, no rest in days,
yet something in you slept like folded cream,
Rose-o'-the-Winds.
You were trying to tell the fruiterer
(she of the grass-green silks and velvets)
that her apples weren't fit for stewing, and she said
'A houseful of helpless weans you've got
they'll do not a hand's turn for you
stuck in that poky wee flat all day
with the door on the chain cause you're
feart of the neighbours. Aye, I know
they buy you flowers, they get them here.'

One day you left a note:
'There's seven dinners in the oven.'
Your hair turned black,
you slimmed into the clothes you used to wear.
You met a stranger in the woods, quite kind at first,
and then he's telling you something about his knife.
You remember an urgent prior appointment.
Then, when you've turned the page
you take a long look at yourself.
The mirror tells you, with regrets,
your newly acquired stepdaughter
is a lot more cute than you. This makes your day
black, or maybe green, but is it middle age? maturity?
It doesn't really matter. Look in the glass:
It says you look just fine, ever after all.

The story's for you, but it isn't yours. Now stop.
Rewind to the tangled forest. Stop.
O see ye not yon narrow road,
so thick beset with thorns and briers?
That is the path of righteousness.

Proceed one hundred yards, and stop.
There's a fork in the road, and a legend etched in stone:
Go this way and lose your life
go that way and lose your mind
Rose-o'-the-Winds. Observe the wych elm
by the path: a bough extends
above your head, and from that bough
a pale hand dangles, nay – gesticulates
(maybe you had seen it); take it
in both of yours, I'll pull you up.

Arjuna and Draupadi in Glasgow

I am the southwest wind
I salt the air and soak the earth.
These ravelled clouds of mine shake out
the tenemental warp and weft
of sulphured sandstone rows.
A rustheap rolls up, bringing you,
you in a saffron thundercloud
your heels that press the ochre boards
as tensile rain hits petals, whose
pubescence tries to hold to it:
those drawn bows.
Here at last I can see neither
bowstring, wrist nor flight, and so
my shot bends like a sleepy fruit
burns along the fuse you lit
to its target: war.

Chemin de la Riole

A particle ploughs silver bromide emulsion
silver precipitate, negative light.
A tunnel of green, or a grey triforium
day in day out. Day in day out
the shoots and spiricles drift,
cloud chamber curlicues construed
in pre-war physics labs, all teak
and brass and streaky skylight.
If grass is traces,
what of? A Douglas fir
rockets from underground.
An oak goes up like a landmine. Beeches
gush in spluttering oil. Slow down.
The woody lungs breathe in
blossom, breathe out, and fall.
A giant redwood treacle telescope slows
the photons down to verbs of motion,
to fulmars that waft off the sun.
Delve darkness, stiffwing, dipping light,
scream off the planet gannetries
and crash in thickets of photosynthesis.

Night, now, the solar wind's recoiled
in dark reactions of antigreen.
Owlets swoop through the wood, neutrinos
slant through ghaists and houlets, rain,
the ground, an army command post, on
to Horizon Depth, where one might
zap a nucleus, unobserved
by gulper eels, whose faint fluorescence
burns the feral circuitry
of sensors built to track and parse
(The hackles rise: there's something out there)
inferences ages with
late Mandelstam and Stony Limits.

Lilac mixes scent into the night
air, that rises off warm droplets

hung on grains of sand from Africa.
Trojan A (Aeneas) hits city C
(Carthage) annihilates Phoenician D
(Dido), decaying into Roman A
and smoke of sandalwood. Exit.
A sandstorm rises and is towed
offshore by the north wind, crossing the Alps
by night, like Hannibal's airforce (the jumbos)
jamming moonlight off the glaciers,
battering Roman lands with all its force,
which is very gentle. Tomorrow –
sand on windscreen wipers,
sand in the magnolia. On the fur of bumble bees,
in carwash rollers. Ampersand in honey.
Silicates in the sweet
buzz of carbonous life.
The Atlas cedar planted by Dido
interprets heaven to the City of God.
Oil reserves are banked in Punic silicon chips.

Where was I? Getting wet, pleased with myself
for not dissolving yet.
For time's the jamjar, gravity's the lid
and water's the universal solvent.
I am an old man
out in the storm
with no umbrella.
Is this in the Confucian sense
where old is wise, umbrella-less
is tough enough to go through chaos
unprotected? Otherwise
these analects are all of me
that will.

Well-read, well-fed, what's the difference?

or

Christians have bagged a lot more lions than the latter have had hot baptised dinners

On reading 'Nut-brown Poet' by Alfred Corn, in Verse

If Ashbery's verse is what survives
translation of Stevens into a strip
where peasant farmers in Martha's Vineyard
cripple pitchforks on mesozoic
mosaics of digitised Judge Dredd,
and there's no more to this than feeling
redeemed, please find returned your special offer.

When the government orders panels for graffitists
and Rauschenberg has to buy De Kooning's
permission before he rubs him out,
when the lion lies down like a lamb,
and reading him can free us from any
responsibility to Truth (p. 28)
I Will Beat Their Heads Into Ploughshares
in the Land of the Living, Saith the Lord
(See Babylon, what's left of it. What was
left of it).

Take this moonshine monstrance,
made for a transuranic twister which is
misconstruing me and you as shadows of itself
no more! It's bound for the ocean deep
where the happy clams, tough mussels and tubeworms
warm to hydrothermal vents,
swap bacteria like old jokes,
fixing hydrogen sulphide to sicken
the hypothetical ragged claws,
the real high-pressure predators.
J. Alfred Corn sleeps with the fishes.
He snores. And snores.

Public Opinion

Well kids, now that we're changing reels
and Roy has commenced his death-defying,
laser-guided leap toward
the scalp of the redskin riding bareback
up the gulch below, I'd like to ask you a question:
should he (a) twist aside and grab that branch
growing from the canyon wall,
avoiding pain to himself and the brave
who is, after all, obeying orders, or
(b) follow through, unseat the Iroquois,
seize the tomahawk wrist with his left
and neutralise with the right? Hands up
if you think that (b)'s the answer.
Hmm, that's INTERESTING. What's that son?
What do you mean you've got a reservation
about the conduct of this survey?

'85% of the British People support the war in the Gulf'
Moskovskie Novosti, 17.2.91

Targeted cohorts and randomised clusters
of folk who subscribe to the phone and the vote are
collected and sorted, recycled and sold.
Mustered at dawn, at stops and stations,
the khaki electorate creases and smooths
its brow, its mucoid camouflage tissues,
its tabloid columns and quality rags.
In infra-red light districts
midnight splatter movies roll.

GVA

Geneva dear you have a woman's name
and today you told me you need me
offering Mt Jallouvre from the railway station
and from the Pont de la machine
on the turning water summits over Flaine
where springs uncurdle in the hanging valley
to aerosol the glacial wall
for history has passed you by
in Nazi gliders closing on Glières
with the traffic in diplomatic plate
you give yourself to me Geneva
no one has loved you like this since Lord Byron.
Slut.

An Amethyst for Horace, his ode IIII, 30*

I've made a monument bigger than Elvis,
slick as a simile, anti-corrosion
guarantee long as the law is enforceable;
gist will survive when the language is lost,
weathering author and inspiration
as long as lives are brought in sacrifice
to death, in which the rose's red
petal is tender as bedsores, death
as a train while the couple steals a last
death that hones the present tense
and the blade sings as it dwindles. Sober up:
nothing anyone ever said
will last as long as I am dead.

---

* It is said that the ancient Greeks believed an amethyst in the wine cup would keep the drinker sober.

———

Here's old Yeno ripping up the rule-book:
all your scrolls and sutras, rags and reason
wrapping paper! Redolent silk! You
put down that
brush I'm not dictating
Ach, let me get my breath back.

On seein 'Penis Envoi' on a contents page an wunnerin whit it cd mean

Go littel prick, lyke tae a cordliss moose,
lee aff the gentle furrow
amid the winter bracken o the mons,
an snoove in every burrow
you kin squeeze or rattle roon in.
Mak mair contax
thn a public libury copy say of
Michael Jackson: the buke o the
film o the tune, or Cawse
ma Politan, or Jings, or Peepil's Fren.
Jist mind y pick up less in the way o
viral anecdotage
on the wey. Dust jaicket, eh?
An whin yir back,
forwandirt and forjaisket
wi makin the maukin ding,
an whin ma liver's back fae Burgundy,
my hert fi the Hielans, ma lungs
fae the laundry, and my brains,
ma squasshy walnut smergh fi its
pickle-jaur in the oaffice,
we'll mibbe can get thegither
an dae organic barbershop quintets
under ur windy. Mibbe she'll gie us
undeclared employment the odd dinnertime,
munelight when the weanzr it school
and the wee yin asleep in iz pram.

Intellectual Property

Review by mechanical private without result,
permission of events unauthorised, current
copyright of photocopying,
reporting of any a be or C
reserved in research or reproduced.
The owners of publishers part (criticism)
the rights and the written part
form, poem, part.
Reproduction reproduced
all permission stored.

The electronic prior in the study
transmitted this poem,
no copyright, no liability or prosecution
retrieval for any written criminal
in this civil system
the poem means
whether otherwise or without
any may any may may be.

Referendum Day 3

Irrefutable, and unconvincing,
said David Hume of Bishop Berkeley's argument
that a tree unseen by anyone in a wood
is undemonstrable and does not exist.
Hume wouldn't let in God for the trees to root in His attention,
nor would he let the leprechaun of reason from his grip,
but the thought that those elaborate dendrological arrangements
were a class that snapped to attention when the teacher turned
                                                    from the board
must have driven him crackers (I can see him in the staffroom).
Don't fret: the raptor that patrols Ben Vorlich
brings great clefts of pine to be as it seeks out other things;
the cushioned thump at the back of the woodpecker's skull,
the stuck of sap when it wags itself like a dog that grips a stick,
the ramp and tilt of slaters in the gullies of its bark
suggest that, yes, the tree is there. Says Berkeley, 'Show it to me!'
I can't. And when I fly away from Scotland,
packing it carefully down in cotton wool for another year,
when I think of it, near as old as any tree,
am I using a Roman stone for a step? Is this the last
light from a done star reeling into my eye like a measuring tape?

Referendum Day 2

Was it Kelvin or Clerk-Maxwell, Satie or Tobias Hume
orchestrated this wee gathering on the darker side of
Metis (one of Jupiter's wee satellites),
up to our ears in aspic, re-rehearsing *Brigadoon*?

It would seem (though I can't say what Dunce or Watt or Michael
                                                          Scot
concocted the theology) that we're staying here
in Corkerhill West – 'a Tibetan assembly' –
until our heirs decide, like, if we are or if we're not.

I mean, severally and jointly are we a nation or a neep?
(Neep! Neep!) This thing's not working! Yogi Bear and his
cheap laser link to the front page of the *Herald*...
Tea break's over: back on your heids.

Referendum Day 1

St Columba voted no
from the orbit of Io
which is where the skilful go
        skating in the autumn.

Scots wha peddled kingdom come
Knox and Marx and opium,
Cattle prods and, eh, the Drum
        birl there in tandem.

Early exit polls from Hell
(... *reel and set, cross and...*) tell
'Don't Think Twice' is doing well
        out of pandemonium.

Did I say Columba neg?
What I meant was good St Meg.
Sub-sub editor, I beg
        take a corrigendum.

Reader, think on them and me,
disenfranchised over sea and time:
we're waiting breathlessly
        on YOUR decision.

Grace

After a week we drove down from the snows
and woke to find primroses in the park behind the house
where, after about ten minutes, she got fed up playing football.
I'm bored, she said, and smiled. Can I climb the cherry tree?
I got her bike from its place in the neighbour's garage
and this time I'd mislaid the pump adaptor:
she must have got to ride it all of a dozen times
since we bought her it three years ago. Three years.
Metabolism takes her at ten metres per second squared
away from me.

Norman MacCaig – For his Eighty-Fifth Birthday

Maybe it's your fine disdain for them
that puts me in mind of Thales the Milesian,
Anaximander watching opposites curdle from the One,
Heraclitus of Ephesus and Fire – all flat earthers,
at home with archipelagoes of planets
and a hebrides of heavy versifiers.

A man in your position
doesn't mummify his metaphors.
You go back a long way, before jazz and the blues
divorced, your words – to when what we know
still lived with who we are; your voice –
to whenever it was the oboe learned to talk.

Whereas it's better to enter the Kingdom of Heaven
missing the offending limb than not at all,
there's some truncations make this life impossible.
That's as it should be.

You wouldn't have wanted to live without your legs.
Under the knife, out on the trolley,
'laughing and joking with the nurses'
as they say,

till the post-op shock had cornered you
and drowned you like a kitten. Up!
on your tip-toes, up! and He'll lift
His Cathie over the Pearly Gates.

I'd just spent an evening keying in names and numbers
to the fax machine
— yours was zero one, by the way.

Well I'm just going to leave it there.
I'll be borrowing your other black tie again;
you'll not ask for it back.

What'll it be now, Patrick? The translator
to make a silk of a sow. Sam Beckett's match
in English words, though not in dervish silence
till now.   In Brazzaville
who'll pay the choirs to wail all night for you?

Sorley Maclean

Wolves or wolfhounds, in the emptiness
– no more reluctance, nothing but the fleet
the fleeting track and melting in the snow
that melded wind and drift for half a breath –
will sport the cross-hairs of this life and death.

Ten Petrarchan Sonnets in a Khoisan Click Language

Ten or was it zen
Petrarchan as in written on the heart
sonnets, sonatas – things that sound
in a place where hunters whisper.

———

The sky was the usual southern mess,
the Cross was down and Canopus rising;
meteorites came crashing into time.
A lonely Chinese restaurant
talk of work and family, time,
the good of verse, analysis,
I didn't see the danger
the spoor of creatures figured in the sky
at noon that lick their paws in the heart
of a candlepod acacia.

At the grave of David Livingstone's infant daughter in the ruins of their house near Gaborone

Lisa, Lizzie, Betsy, Beth,
a stony dream, an early death,
your mummy's gone and this is the hand that rocks you.

Elizabeth in this place
the full futility of talking
has dried my lips until they crack in song.

Sophia

'We believe what eases our minds'
John Anderson

Before Martha was Martha
before Martha was born
in crystal Geneva
I heard a ship's horn
bring in the New Year.

I heard hundreds of vessels
that weighed on the Clyde
that my grandfather plated
and my father sighed over
at work. Can you hear it?

A jig on the pedals
of thirty-foot pipes!
Here, open the window –
frost in the pines.
We were 500 miles from the water.

I was 500 mile from the ocean
where a great river runs
out of steam, out of breath
in a wheeling and rusting
and shuddering life.

I'd just chased a wolf-spider
from under my net,
I'd got under the blankets
and put out the light
when I heard them – all

the gougers and biters,
anaesthetists, all
that the bats couldn't glean
from the thatch or the wall,
and I waited.

Now the south wind draws snow
from the Drakensberg Ridge
and the rains can come fast
as the plummeting edge
of a snake-eagle's wing.

Well it drowned out their chatter
and maybe drowned them,
and I slept like a babe.
It was wind in the palms,
wind in the branches

and clattering leaves.
I was far from the ocean
and miles from the sea
but I thought I heard You...

Happy the Pure in Heart

Two of us were standing at the office door
when here come Sorgho down the corridor
looking like he's making headway
against a strong south-westerly.
'Heureux les coeurs purs' he snapped, and on he went.
By and by he's coming back,
still shouldering into that wind.
'Now who was that intended for?'
'Moi-même' he grinned, head down. Well brother, maybe,
but given your track record
you have to mean pure crazy.

———

Stuffing a payphone on the border
for some place five-and-a-half time zones away
to clicks and pauses that gulp numbers
as limbic signals drop from one
expectancy to none –
linoleum
in limbo
and my hands have lost their memory. As for this –

Well it looks like butchered bagpipes, and it feels
like they've been stepped on, but
it dunders the beat
like a Strathclyde Police pipe band.

All or None

The fact, discovered by Bowditch, that the heart muscle, under
whatever stimulus, will contract to the fullest extent or not at all
Dorland's Medical Dictionary

There's collarbones like hickory wands,
fine as fanstruts on a soundboard,
patient as wingstruts, fuselage
to vellum stretched on a warping frame.
I could lock you away in this desk drawer
with nothing but the desk drawer key for company.
God knows why I put up with you. God knows
why a woman should take the weight
the aches and murmurs of a husband.

Paludrine

You have a sense of the absurd, but you don't like the absurd.

Well I don't think I was bitten
and transmission's slow in winter
and there's drug-resistant strains there anyway,
so I stopped taking the pills, my wee Pals,
because they cloud the vision
and dull the hearing, and disable
my Houdini sense of humour,
which I need now. Besides,
what's good enough for Dante and MacDiarmid
will do for me.

The Firefinch (M.C.)

Smokey's after the firefinch. Listen, cat:
you touch that bird and you'll be feeding
the Gucci golfbags in the creek.
I love it more than all the flocks
that cross the desert with the clouds.
It's molten rock, the tiny
pulse of possibility. It is
the loving breath that breathes on me.

———

Nearly there. Now you've recovered faster
than from flu or any faint
indisposition.
There's nothing can crack your heart
when you don't own one:
you're a Christian saint,
you're a Zen master.

Poinsettia

Yesterday there swam in the lamplight
purposeful as a fossil ammonite
moving me to guess what it might be
a fallen leaf curled in on its palm
and puckered sideways, toward the thumb
to duck the light and cowl the damp.

Boxed in their crimson prime last month
the veins of the leaf are warping, wiry
ribs and rungs on the ingrown gangway
of a spiral galleon that'll never
right its rigging or explain itself to me.

Stigma

Leaves graze and assuage the sunlight. Raptors
quarter the moor and cauterise.
Our insomniac senses, though,
like gnats, the Pleiades, open secrets,
drain and drown the world in its sleep:
it all relaxes into us
like blowback on a hypodermic.

Sorrow's a cup that's never done:
a circle floats to the perfect brim
and spills a hare-lip, dribbling,
a ruptured hydrant roaring, then
the pavement tilts and founders. Dawn
and the skyline's sunk,
my lungs are pondweed.

Strangler Fig

It reaches down from somewhere in the leafage
as if big jugs were pouring down cement
that braids and melds about the bole.

When the Hottentot Queen was turned into a tree by Prester John
an elephant that went to scratch its back against her skin
was promptly melted by the sun god Ra for that great sin
and strung out like a boneless pietà: that's aetiology.

A message in a cleft stick quote I am
no parasite unquote. Anacreontic cicadas
eat more than me. I live on air
and dirt. I am a pin-up
that the model won't live up to – a cover story
over the event. I do not steal. I own
no real estate, but ancient lights.
I rise in welts on many backs
and flex like ice in drainpipes.

Tristia (Black Sea Blues)

A lover and a father and a daughter (not yours) all dead
and your own along the shore
is finding relics and remainders.
There you're standing on the sea floor
looking up. You don't want to post that letter.
Shored in a house with the red cross crew
she's lulled to sleep by the waves and gunfire.
Farther off, beside the point,
there's Phoolan Devi, the bandit queen.

Mayday

A fruit tree crackled up from sleep
and blossom hung about like thunder
grey in the April snow, repeat:
grey in the April snow.

From the Sanskrit

We give an example of an ekaksara *stanza, employing only one consonant throughout:*
>   *Dadado dudda-dud-dadi*
>   *dadado duda-di-da-doh*
>   *dud-dadam dadade dudde*
>   *dad'-adada-dado 'da.dah*

Did I do Dido? Wd I dodo
DD? Do IOU a dead id?
D-day, de-wedded, I did dhow.
'Aid Dido, dude', ode daddy added,
Aideed'd aid Aida'.
                                    Da?
You'd owe a dewy-eyed ode, ide-oid.
Adieu. A dowdy odd doe O-D'd.

Artou/ Off the Map

In the map shop the music playing
was John Coltrane so far away
So far away, some rag-top Rolls
of a raindance raga, Indian English plosives
in the tabla's Vedic commentary.

The map I took to be Tamil Nadu
explained itself as Hindu Kush
(as fingerprinted by the Swiss).
As I looked down, to touch the names
in the folds of Kashmir beaten in lines

by nimble hooves and bangled heels,
Srinagar joined Schiehallion
(the first hill caught in contours), Lochnagar
and every trait I'd flatten out, beyond my span
of days for sensing the ribcage rise, a country's cadences.

Due to this earth quake hit lakhs of people
had been lost their family member their shelter,
they are in very drugedy condition.
Most of the people have lost their hands, legs eyes,
and were hardly injured. This seems to us very sad
and undiagestable.

We write this letter with tears of lakhs of people
this quake hit really affected 5 Districts.
In these affected area
6 villages are our service area in this six village
95% of the buildings and thacted roofs and were fully destroyed
and they lost their all materials,
these affected people were needy of MEDICAL FIRST AID,
food and shelter, at least temporary huts,
clothes, foods, medical treatments. Many families have lost
their heads (Husband or wife) many children lost both
their father and mother, we also write this letter with tears.

From the Metaforest

Brahman denotes the term to be defined
and âtman that which defines it;
by Brahman the limitation implied in âtman is removed,
and by âtman the conception of Brahman as
a divinity to be worshipped is condemned.

I have studied, most reverend sir,
the Rigveda, Yajurveda, Sâmaveda,
the Atharvaveda as fourth, the epic
and mythological poems as fifth veda,
grammar, necrology, arithmetic, divination,
chronology, dialectics, politics, theology,
the doctrine of prayer, necromancy, the art
of war, astronomy, snake-charming and the fine arts, –
these things, most reverend sir, have I studied;
therefore am I, most reverend sir,
learned indeed in the scripture,
but not learned in the âtman.
Yet I have heard from such as are like you
that he who knows the âtman vanquishes sorrow.
I, however, most reverend sir, am bewildered.
Lead me then over, I pray,
to the farther shore that lies beyond sorrow.

Variations for Richard Peck

On Monday 9 June Mr Richard Peck, a specialist in diarrhoeal
                     diseases with the World Health Organization
Jumped into the Ganges after a ten-year-old child who was in
                               difficulty.
The body of Mr Peck was found on Friday, thirty-five miles
                             downstream.
The body of the child has not yet been recovered.

Ah but it was a reckless thing to do:
The surface turns as slow as an old LP
But in there even a sinking stone
Will float like a tone-arm.

Roped up on a ridge of wind and gravity I asked
What if I slip? – You won't – All right, what if *you*
Slip? – If I fall off one side
You must jump off the other side at once.

According to Herodotus one King Cyrus of Assyria
Lost a favourite horse to the river as he marched on Babylon.
He exacted prompt revenge by having his army dig 180 channels
                           on either side, to kill its force
Then he went on to take Babylon. God has done the same to
                               poetry.

Heraclitus somewhere says that all things are in process and nothing
                               stays still
And likening existence to the stream of a river he says
That you would not jump twice
Into this same river.

As raindrops hit the navy-blue plastic cloth on the table outside
They send across the puddles little grey ball-bearings of water
That last as long as meteors,
Long as the surface tension holds.

Camus somewhere writes of a girl at the parapet of a bridge;
A man walks by and hears a splash as she jumps off.

At another point a man is standing on a bridge,
Startled by a disembodied laugh.

A great bag of water will form
On the leaf of a nasturtium
Then fall.
The leaf springs up like a branch when a pigeon has gorged itself
                                        on plums and fluttered off.

A little bird skewers the Ganges with fire,
Hefts it up
And drowns it in the air.
A corpse gets bobbed under then burned on the ghats.

A jasmine
Garland sinking
After you in stinking
History.

Alexander the Great in the Hindu Kush
Played by Richard Burton ('No, not yet!')
A voice that howled for resonance in the Welsh hills
Dies out between the Jura and the Alps.

Ganges – you'd say the name of a Greek god,
But she's a mother goddess.
Negative theology:
Take leave of your mind and dive into the dark.

If the Bodhisattva knew all things (including the one who knows)
                                        to be unreal,
The adjectival saviour of virtual beings from no danger,
This life no more than a juggle of statistics,
Why should he leave the cusp of an empty flood to rescue me?

Truth is sunk
In information,
Justice
In good offices.

The Ganges as a holy song above the mountain
Set out in a great scroll by the Gomukh glacier,
Expanded to several volumes in Varanasi,
With chemical and cloacal marginalia taking over.

The flux – the river as some unclean intestine
And the way to cope with it no wonder drug
But clean water, a little sugar and salt,
Patience and a kind word. You were the kind word.

The hiatus as the cord snakes out before you
The echo of a shout

No rainy Sunday afternoons left for you Mr Richard Peck
No memory no reflection.
You decided in one moment who you are; you staked your life
on it
And won.

Arabesque

Limber, remember, reconcile
The given grammar to the breaks
In breath, in rhythm,
To the shape that takes
You and gives
Everything but the wings your muscles conjure.

The triple grand jeté and arabesque
That gave the great man pause for half a second
Showed twelve long years' devotion to the dance:

For linear
Rise in quality
Rise in cost is exponential.

Who's kidding who? I know
Your feet are killing you. I see
Your lungs strain, and you're slippery with sweat.
I bet you'll down a litre
At the pit-stop in the wings.

Is there any discernible point to this at all?
This emptying of gesture till there's nothing and it hurts?

My thanks to Silhouette and Léotard for showing you
Reach for the light
As though your whole self burgeoned
From that glorious little bush
As though man's ultimate desire in seeing the dance
Was to roll over and snore.

Style is the simplicity with which a difficult thing is done
But when the difficult task itself is style,
When beauty is the goal, the artisan
Can know too much. The fall, when the leaf turns,
Is nothing. When the bud unwinds
When the dancer when
The dancer is
The dance.

Adolesce

As we got to the first floor landing I asked you out.
You smiled and said no, you had to meet your cousin.
I was glad you had a cousin. I was glad grey light
had moored the banister.
Tenements were sandstone, that I knew,
but I wondered what stone the steps were –
grey as light, worn as driftwood beams,
as lips or shinbones I could have kissed,
like the lintel of a shore temple,
caressed and corroded by winds and visitors.

Grand Hotel

A 20 dollar room
a 19 dollar call to say
I'm back to piped hot water
optional kick-start air con.
and the vagaries of the telephone.

I won't say
the SHELL building by the catwalk
has a big red neon sign with the 'S' conked out
that the air would kill a cockroach
that the breakfast garden's bleary and cloaked in soot.

The place is perfect.

Die the Death

'With the delegates sat there like a choir of jam jars
he dropped this ring in my hand without a glance
as he got up and walked towards their captain
saying maybe we could talk this out. And that, of course,
was the last of him till he turned up in the market
under the butcher's stall. I believe the ring's for you.'
                    Or:
took two in the gut at a time and place in town
where even strays would have had ulterior motives.
One journalist maintains it was for lines
on gullets slit for 'la francophonie'.
The coroner found hookworm. His widow
found grandchildren, but orphaned, and her son
didn't know what to do with the African statues,
cheap copies that they were, in rotten wood.

On Reading John Berryman's
'Eleven Addresses to the Lord'

John Henry, Cardinal Bones, if I can't pray
I'll write my wrongs as you did. Intercede
for me when I succeed you on that day
to the howling chair, where I maun chafe and bleed
till you — word, voice and corpse as never broken,
swack and singing glory karaoke —
don't make me laugh.

Presto!

Bury my heart in Partick, it'll rise on Brigton, bleary,
to see the rain fall on the dirty water.
Plant it in Kelvingrove, it'll sprout
a crop of Rubik cubes. In vitro
watch it split and multiply,
divide and conquer. At conkers
it won't crack or need a vinegar marinade,
or those wee sappy spikes. Try it with onions
to sweeten it and help you shed a tear.
Take it to Presto: you could shy it
at tins on the top shelf; play keepie-up
when queueing at the check-out. It's free
from pain and guilt; there's only puzzlement at beating
the opposition
                    never stood a chance.

Poems never written down
pebbles in the ocean's throat
Lagavulin's tawny shine
claret's memories of oak
that never took to shingle beach
or saw its seasoned rings would rhyme
in rosined ships, in reels of mine;
we're fiddles sunken in their song
from peg to bridge, across the briny
ocean-o to Capricorn
from Uist, garrisoned with sheep
and two-and-twenty (count them) years
asleep in postcards. Out of the blue
a curving swell will hit the shore
from blistered winds in extasy
that none survived, or no one knew.

A4ism

I unplug the lamp,
connect a kettle
of water enough for one cup,
sit down to A4 in the grey light
and wait.

When the window clouds, I give the mug
a bag of China black, whose blue paper pouch
dangles overboard on its twine.
'Congo' is also a Chinese tea,
from 'kung hu', the work in making it:
argosies of paper,
leaves of light.

With the water poured, the air in the bag
is almost enough to float the teaspoon,
stainless steel on delft. Clink.

I take the teabag on the spoon
and wind them both in the twine, to squeeze out
the darkest of the tea. 'Theism' –
maybe that's my problem.

The litter bin's two yards away.
I lob the teabag, rarely miss
the bin, or the pouch that flutters out
like the pennant on a horseman's back
in Kurosawa's *Ran*. Poor man!
Never a woman but Lady Macbeth;
that's not been my experience. Listen:
offer me a front-row seat in heaven now
in exchange for the rest of my life,
which (I would guess) will not improve. You *know*
what I would say.
                    My dear,
for all the tea in China.

TANTRIS

I

At dawn, a skiff was found in coastal waters,
one man on board, who said he'd give his name
to the king of the land, no less. In spite of orders
we landed him. He sings with might and main
      as though a song would stanch
      the rotten artery in his thigh.

What is the question? That is the question. Moped
and moaned, I did, through quest and antiquest
in search of the existential hot potato
to trans-substantiate my cranial lead
      to cordial gold, denier
      that desire would inter

myself, my sober clarity, inter
this Don Quixote riding on a moped
as Nero fiddled for a last denier.
An answer without a question, antiquest
      I am, a slinging lead,
      a blighted lazy-bed potato.

Consider the thumping heart as a potato
that sprouts in the buttonhole. Now disinter
and stop the gap with counterweights of lead
and a 50cc motor from a moped:
      the finest, the antiquest
      you can find for five denier.

I'll spin you then a yarn of any denier
you want, and sing to you with all my potato
or heart or two-stroke motor. Antiquest
is all, or all I care for. Inter-
      est is mine. O faithful moped,
      come and we'll souse the place in lead.

Now: punctuate a polisman with lead?
or charm a damsel out of her ten-denier
silk whispers? Throttle out of my moped
the QUESTION whose answer is potato?
		Dilemmas of an inter-
		national civil antiquest.

Religion? I have followed the antiquest
upstream and down as far as they would lead,
lead me, at least. Now, in the inter-
regnum, I've reasoned with the best. My last denier
		gone. *Tremor potato-*
		rum, drunk in charge of a moped.

		– Sing yo-ho-ho for Potato Rum Shakes, the boatman,
the àntiquest denier mopèd thus.
He'll soon be lapped in lead – that's *inter nos.*
We'll take him to the port authority doctor
		and maybe a blast of ether
		will stop him ranting on the way.

His name is apparently Tantris (superscript one)
though Tantris what (superscript two) we don't know.
		– Here's a phone book: pick one the monu-
mental sculptor won't mis-spell.
		Note one: this would seem to be Pictish. Footnote
		two: Tantris MacDuff.

Tantris MacDuff?
				– That'll do… am I no deid yet?
or are you St Boutros?
				– No, I'm Doctor Smee;
now tell me, Tantris…
				– First name terms already?
That's odd, I don't remember swiving you.
		Here, give me a sick line, pal, I need
		the best specialist in town.

I have heard tell of an excellent first lady
in this republican rhotic jamboree
of a popular united democratic
etcaetera who might know how to deal
        with the haematoxic curse I caught
        from this interesting blade.

I'm also told she's a razor-keen collector
of villanelles, slip-jigs and roundelays:
the sort of thing your dawn patrol here's humming
because they missed the lyrics. Trouble is
        who gets the blame if you nail down
        the musical box's lid?

In first and ambulance driver's gear and haar
as blank as empty paper I parole
along a road remembered or freshly tarred
from fantasy (you'd think I ought to know which)
        but wipe away my breath:
        a scribble of branches, hedges, halt.

It says halt.
                — Well halt then, eejit! Wind it down.
Wind down the window. Officer! Good day!
We have an authorisation, here it is.
Could I ask you please to point that thing away?
        Sure, point it at the driver,
        by all means. Thank you. Good day.

Drive on. And by the way, you see those rosebeds?
Well if you hear a motorcade, drive on in:
it's them or us. The aerial outriders
come round that hill like wind announcing rain.
        If you stop at the old portcullis
        we can stretcher him in from there.

           – If I stop at the old portcullis? If I stop
and turn around, he's dead, I lose my job.
If she learned what his living does to her life,
that, too, would be end of story, out of work.
           We take him up the stairs
           to her. A word, if she were wise:

'Your daughter, what's her name, love's fair signet
with which in days to come his heart was sealed
and locked from all the world save her alone...'
Wait! Ask him, if he's forty days adrift
           since he took that wound, how he can say
           'No treatment seems to work'?

Eh? Poison him and poison your existence.
Give him the antidote and he will dote
but not on you, whose honour will prevent you
repaying one who must dishonour and
           bereave you, without malice. It's
           too late. The singer, ma'am.

           – You ask for a song: I'm more than glad to give it.
You are alive and I am nearly dead.
Your face is brown and bright as any icon.
Love gathers with a lifting of the head
           in winter, dawning red
           from Thunder Bay to the Yukon.

But you are alive and I am nearly dead,
me: chic and shabby in my shiny suede
with all the prospects of a tappit chicken.
Love gathers with a lifting of the head?
           Not this one: A to Z
           amours neglect me as I weaken.

You are alive and I am nearly dead
from charging in where angels know to tread
the footbrake. Near the end of my declension
love gathers with a lifting of the head.
           My soul is in the shredder
           and although my senses thicken,

Though you are alive and I am nearly dead,
love gathers, with a lifting of the head.
Your majesty, madame, a wee Glenlivet...
I beg your pardon, Mrs President,
        I'm sorry, after singing, though,
        my throat gets awful dry.

        – I'll give you no more poison. You poor minstrel,
you have a poisoned wound!
                        – That would be why
no treatment seems to work.
                        – But I can cure you;
take heart! You'll teach my daughter what you sing!
        The ambulancemen can go.
        This draught will make you sleep for a week.

        – To sleep for a week? To sleep, perchance to dream?
        Now THAT's the game. To dream of being asleep,
alive to my oblivion as the sandman
my stupid selves doth severally sap
        and carry off like carpets
        till the driftwood fire's so low

on the river bend, that the salient conflagration
of neighbouring stars is all but audible;
on a pantry shelf in my Palladian villa,
in the saddle, fo'c'sle, belly of a whale,
        on a mattress, ledge or rug,
        a billiard table – anywhere

will do.
        – He was a long time going under.
A player, to the callused fingerpads.
Life's salted down or it's gathered in the fingertips,
in panic buds, on peaks above the flood
        with a force and independence
        more than music could control.

PORT AUTHORITY RECORD: T. MACDUFF,
MISPRIZEN FOR A BARD AND SET ADRIFT
IN A CURRAGH BY THE PIRATES WHO DESPOILED
HIS ARGOSY SIX WEEKS AGO – they were right:
>   this fellow's not a merchant,
>   but he's more rather than less.

The flayed piper of Harmelin, I presume.
>   – You what?
>   – I said a week; you slept three days.
>   – Your laudamay had a wee bit too much water.
>   – What manner of merchandise had you on board?
>   – To tell you that I'd have to start
>   with how the freight was fraught.

So: *How The Freight Was Fraught* On Saturday mornings
or: *How The Wrest Was Wrought* I'd lie in state
top bunk, my brother and sister filed below me
in beds I'd got when the hospital shut down
>   and stare at the plaster cornice
>   a yard or so above my head:

as wide as the billet, detail drowned in gloss;
all I could see was the L-shaped bit that ran
from what we had of a window we couldn't open
along the original lathe and plaster wall.
>   Our home was just that sliver
>   of a tremendous wedding cake –

I wanted more. The King sits in Dunfermline
toun drinking the cheap red, drinking the bluid-red wine.
It's whaur will I get a guid sailor to sail this
whack fol the diddle-o dandy ship o mine?
>   Well it's up and spak an elder knicht
>   aw wait a minute, no…

A terrible place it is for ritual boasting,
the city and state: the prosperous convene
to bum about who they diddled in the city chambers,
to talk up their investments, to inflate
     their reputation. Youngsters
     crow about their youth. The wise

will talk with respect about their aging parents.
The idiot boasts of his beautiful young wife.
The flunkeys flit along the banqueting tables
like fingers on a fretboard. Claret? Trifle?
     I didn't have a look in:
     cost a lottery or a life.

Without a notion vague what I was after,
I took a psaltery down to the shore.
The rattling tide rolled up like sarky laughter
without a notion vague what I was aft-
     er; the cruit was my craft,
     aye, and it roiled the ocean floor

without a notion vague what I was after.
I took a psaltery down to the shore:
like King Canute, St Francis and MacDiarmid
I'm talking to the waves, the wolves, the wall,
     without a busker's permit
     like a king or saint or hermit

insisting on the earth that I'd inherit,
Davidic victory or Orphic fall.
Like King Canute, St Francis or MacDiarmid
I'm talking to the waves, the wolves, the wall:
     what character has risen
     like the language to a song?

What Willie Graham from a whisky prison,
what creature's breath and braided scales, arisen
in frisky foam, a wolf in woolfell, buzz
in trumpet marine, to the dulcimer and gong,
     what character is risen
     like the language to a song?

When I got home that night, my little sister
was old and grey in worn mourning clothes.
'You've seaweed in your hair' she said, and told me
the city chamberlain had come around
      and served a fiddler's bidding
      to the grand financiers' lunch.

The grand financier!… Where did your lovely curls go
my little one?… Is there anything to eat?
The cowgate, market stalls and crates had nothing but
the usual veg., in the leavings of the light.
      Flea market economy! Even
      the people here look second-hand.

I did see, though, a crowd of burghers roaring
fit to burst with laughter at some poor
spastic smirking to himself and twitching
his chest and elbows. Bodies moved aside
      and I saw he was working marionettes
      that sprang and danced a jig.

And I thought, we're such a bunch of bloody cripples:
wooden levers wedged under the chin,
twisted tubes in mouths in faces twisted
in rage or grief that the keys had locked us in
      to the instruments and wouldn't let us
      leave till we had paid

in blood, of course. I'll show them who's the cripples,
I thought – and did so, at the famous lunch.
The place was chuck-a-brick with old rotarians,
non-executive wretches, boom and crunch
      or crash manipulators
      when I settled down to play

nothing: one of those blanks. A bird was singing
no problem whatsoever as the talk
died down around me, only an ancient mariner
with an upland accent droning on and on.
      My heart was pumping something like
      four dozen beats to the bar

then oh it hit the liftshaft. Breathe in deeply,
don't hold it breathe out slowly, flutter and thump
again. Some syncopation! In the kitchen
a dinnerplate pagoda hit the deck:
      discord on the top two octaves,
      forte. Fine! the keyboard works

(you never can tell on gigs with no rehearsal).
The talker dried as he heard me do his voice
$_{ddd}{}^{di}$ da, $_{ddd}{}^{di}$ da (left thumb and index)
and the starling in the plane tree ^{ha} ha $_{HAA}$
      a theme it had likely copied
      from the clocktower. As it may

be as it may that be that as it may
I was off on a recognisable melody
they recognised! No sooner said and stated
than gone among the grace notes. With my knee
      I chuffed the nether regions
      of the instrument. My right

hand spangled on its own way, and I let it
not know what the left was doing; I knew though,
for I watched it so it never left the register:
the only way I had to keep control
      of rhythms that would loosen bolts.
      They lapped it up. It went

chuff/chuff/shuffle/walk-walk-don't walk-stride-/shuffle/
shuffle/cough/truffle/snuff/-I-in-sin-sain-saint
'my brother hand's got that hoary glossolalia!'
-slàinte-slanted-slated-sated-sate-sat-at-a-la
      /shuffle/-lan-plan-plane-planet 'Would you look at those'
      -plant-pant 'keyboard grins!'

pan-an-/chuff/-a-ad-fad-fade-frayed 'They've got claret'
fraynd-freud-/shuffle/ 'but it's spilling all down their chin.'
feud-oid-id 'I believe they just can't handle
their' /shuffle/chuff/ 'cutlery'/truffle/snuff/. I was in!
      It was homage to catatonia
      for the burghers every night.

From then on I was such a well-paid piper
that within one year it was I who called the tune
and beat the fiddlers at their own inventions.
As I went from mother's pride to mother's ruin
          I boasted I could buy up
          all the merchandise in town.

'You're on.' 'How much?' I struck the oaken table
laden like a river barge with meat and drink
and I bet, to boot, the chiselled floor and corbel
(stopping short of timber, game and mineral rights)
          and swore I'd have for sundown
          all the goods on sale at dawn.

Next day I bought yarn of tram silk, whelks and whetstones,
wrestling rings, torque meter wrenches, tang,
vellum, venom, vaulting blocks and turbans,
truffles, trumpets, truncheons, tubers, tubes,
          sockets, socks and switches,
          throats,
                    – Throats?!
                              – Throats, opoponax,

incense, incunabula, jams and jackets,
hats, harps, harpoons and harpsichords, glycerol, glue,
regulators, reliquaries, pudding,
pear pips, pit props, and – what do you call dried plums?
          – Prunes.
                    – Prunes, yes, groats and grindstones,
          bear fat, bone fat, slitter and scran,

brine and brimstone, cases, corrydander,
axe heads, axle-boxes, ratchel salt,
oxter pickle, haver-straw, earth colours,
catalogues, mung beans, alluvium,
          then one of the merchants asked
          if I had met Boo-Bull Mahoun.

The moss on the wooden pier was just emerging,
the sun was swollen, the evening wind was up,
a line of smoke rose steadily from his hookah
where Boo-Bull sat cross-legged on a mat;
      the only furniture in the room
      was a large red lacquered chest.

I'd been taking stock all day, so what I saw in it
was papers, ledgers, a bamboo-joint inkstand,
pens, rice, dahl, ghee, curry powder, a bamboo pillow,
and yellow shoes with long points like rats' tails,
      but don't mistake a mason
      for a chisel vendor. No,

what Boo-Bull had he usually sold for silver
that he converted into Company bills;
one bill paid the consignor, while the silver
returned to buy teas for the Company,
      which brought in cash to back the bills
      so Boo-Bull bought some more

till at length − that very day − there rode at anchor
a cargo of lead-sealed gunny sacks. In each
a chest of mango wood containing thirty
four-pound cricket balls of opium.
      It was in town, but if I
      landed it, I'd land in jail.

The game was up. I parted with my mansion,
left word to sell the inventory I'd bought,
paid Boo-Bull cash for his shipment. He was gracious
enough to throw in container and crew for nought.
      We caught the ebb. That was that.
      Now what you've got is what you see.

      − In answering me you've raised another question:
what made you want to do the merchants down?
It wasn't enough for you to be that much richer:
you clearly wanted to consume and kill
      their living. What had they done to you
      to deserve that?
            − Lady, it's late,

and you've asked a bitter question, that I'll answer
only because you have tried to save my life.
I wanted more. We had just the top tier corner
of a tenemental wedding cake. Our right
      was to as much space for each of us
      as the three of us had at all.

They offered double, out of town: two-thirds
of what they owed. The other tenants went,
the other communal flats and sublets emptied;
the council repossessed the tenement
      to tart up, or they would have done
      had I not stood my ground.

I wanted more. My brother and sister loved it:
I played piano in the drawing room
(we'd kicked down the partitions) noon till evening
while they explored the draughty, echoing block.
      The boy went through a balustrade
      six floors up. Bad workmanship.

Bad luck. 'Dear Sir,
      In view of circumstances',
they wrote to me, meaning his death, 'your claim
to extra living space is not admissible.
Our offer stands.
      Yours Faithfully'
                  – Please stop.
      It's late, as you say. Before you meet
      my husband, you should rest.

He was playing keyboards in a room he recognised.
He slammed a chord and went straight through the floor:
piano, stool and all. He kept on playing.
Fortissimo! like a shell through joist and board,
      ash soundproofing and ceiling
      he and the lacquered grand went down.

The ash took time to settle. He looked up
and saw he had come through four or five such floors.
This time the Persian rug he was on was hammocked
with the weight. There was nothing under it at all:
      the rug was held at the edges
      by the furniture, to wit:

a couch, a roll-top bureau and a dresser,
a double wardrobe and a library.
He played on, but the silence underneath him
was vast. Was he on the lantern of a dome
      or cupola? *Rallentando. Piano.*
      Pedal. Double F.

II

After such a night! An iron bothy –
I'd smashed its rafters to feed ginger tom,
who purred and flashed around the walls, and embered.
Scuttling rats. A pale thread at the door jamb
      like torches outside. I thought
      they had come to finish me off,

so – grabbed a stave and rushed outside: the Hunter
(couldn't catch a cold), an aspirin moon,
a city on the coast. Among the islands,
too far to hear or smell, the lightning browsed.
      Cuchulain? Even he'd not
      take a stick to a thunderstorm,

And I'll not sort my life out with a pencil,
No matter. And I'll not write to you,
but for you. Long since, when your mother cured me
of harm she'd done, I crossed the powers that be.
      In the dark of subsequent
      events, that does come back to mind...

Red carpet. Twenty acrobats. Circus music.
But all of them packing heat and looking round.
The life president is laughing with his council:
this seems informal. 'Who elected you?'
            (Gauche, I admit.) A gesture
            indicated the councillors.

'And who elected them?' That was unforgivable;
I put it down to nerves. A frozen smile
(three rows of teeth, I swear) for all the council
but not for me. I was glad when we sat down:
            it meant I wasn't expected to
            stretch out on the serving dish.

Twelve at table. Thirteen. Twelve. Among them
one dwarf, two women and a quadruped.
Executive muscle; bruised, blazoned clothing
of adjectival skin. The daylight slaked
            in lymph and opalescence.
            Even the bowl of fruit looked butchered.

To the test: 'If Transit be your name, are you
a Tectosage?'
            'Call me Tantris. I am from
the City and State.'
                        'We've been there!' (Each of them
employed the royal plural.) 'Just before
            the curfew is lifted in the
            chloral dawn you're drifting down

To the mangrove in a grand canal canoe
that unzips the silent wavebands. Like a taupe
silk dress. We pass that Carolingian church;
black waters about the frescoes gulp and purl,
            we lurch: a crocodile collides
            amidships. Bang! These shoes?

We had them made right there. What craftsmanship!
What fees! But what a place!'
                                        'An epiphyte
on brackish waters shored against the sea',
as I said, 'in architectural anagrams
          on bone-thin marble bits, aye,
            whose every surface knows the wind

or did. Medusa, glyphs and hieroglyphs,
hieratic poses in the dance
of lovely dancers held in the friezes, or just
cut stone in its molecular mystery,
          built up in stanzas, silences,
          possessed or left alone.

But who will pay, said Nation A, the plumber?
Who'll buy peripheral history to confirm
some malcontents in palaces? Not A. They need
a theme park. Let the sea wall go. Condemn
          the dead. How about some hippos
          in congested lung canals?

Lacking anything that might compare
with these analects of our history
they trash it, tartanise it, double click
on **this will end your session**. Cries of foul
          when we evict their factors
          they start to shell.'

          'We know of ethnic strife, ridiculous
and mortal. But ecospheres transcend the rifts
in history.'

                    'Oh no they don't. Can you tell me
the difference between Nations A and B?'
          'Nation A likes animals? No one else
          has heard of Nation B?

A an island, B a peninsula?'
                              'Close!
It's that B knows there is a difference, but
has never seen old Nation A does not…
but this is micropolitics, excuse me,
              the sort of thing you bomb with
              party tricks at Hogmanay.'

'Teddy bears!' they grinned.
                              'Why soft toys?'
              'Because we do not like to see a child
destroyed.'
              'Who does?'
                              'You do.'
                                        'THEY do, and you
could have spiked their guns.'
                              'Our people do not love
              your own as much as their sons.'
                                        'That
              I can understand, but why?…'

       'What do you do if a wild and wounded animal
threatens you? What do you do? Of course
you cauterise or slaughter; option A
is risky, B no longer popular. So
              change the metaphor, seek out
              a different strategy.

On the dark side of the planet, rents are cheap,
life cheaper still, and much of our consumption
is mined or nurtured, worked or woven there.
Compunction was a rare commodity
              on the sunny side until a recent
              run of factory fires:

strident calls for reform (Uncharacteristically
the buildings hadn't blown up or burned down,
but all inside had choked, some chained to the bench,
all arthritic, stunted, − and all children.)
              For now, the matter sticks
              in our consumers' collective craw.

What could we do with the hecatombs of retail
that we were widowed with when the music stopped?'
      'Dump it?'
              'On you.'
                    'Why thanks.'
                              'It stopped you thinking
of war; it silenced the tanks.'
                    'No it didn't: folk thought
      'What they offload will corrupt
      or explode'; it rotted in the rain.

It's all connect and control, divide and conquer,
cold calculus in everything you do.'
      'Tantris, you misjudge us: we separate
our trash, we separate our powers; cash
      is kept in blind trust, innocent
      as the flowers. Do you know

we even paid for a poultry farm in your place?'
      'The Horseman's?'
                    '... you know him?'
                            What's the harm
I thought, in letting them know I know something
they don't. Out over silence's crevasse
      and the ice of fremt attention
      here we go. And with just enough rope.

'The Horseman was a prince among us. Many
hoped he would lead them from disgrace. But this
became known. He was relieved of his responsibilities:
phoney charges; house arrest – and time
      to think what to do and time to plan out
      how it ought to be done.

Food: there are those who live on rotten garbage
and it all, or nearly, feeds intestinal worms.
Your capital got all the chickenwire and chickens,
and that got him permission to tour the land
      showing folk what to do with pullets. Also,
      under an alias

he organised, in case the ruling junta
should risk a plebiscite; it did: he won.
There won't be many ministers have received you
with bantams busy as trying on fur coats
          a-clucking about the yard? Just one?
          Well that would be him. Took wing

a day before the coup; he and the president
holed up in a loft. But both their wives were caught.
The soldiers tortured and shot the Horseman's woman;
the other hugged his son, and persuaded them
          she wasn't worth the bullets –
          indeed, they were saving them for her man.

It was time to edit out the opposition.
You make rotten boroughs of thrawn electoral wards
by giving grenade launchers to the national guardians
who kill until folk decide to brave the brunt
          and learn exploding bullets can't
          be used at point-blank range.

Just like the row round here the other morning:
a cat had caught an old crow, maybe broken its wing.
It would hirple off like a cantilevered penguin
humping a bag of spuds. The cat would pounce,
          pin it down again and go back to
          pumicing its paws.

But meanwhile the crows were clotting the capillaries,
so when they got a quorum, down they went
like scissors in crepe, like clapped-out starting motors.
Pussy's put to flight. The old one's off
          again, white feathers spread
          like a hand of cards. Sweet like a crow.

The junta said it was for negotiation.
Who with? Your man had the advantage of not being dead.
No rancour, no intemperate answers. Spooked them
but they needed a figleaf or a figurehead.
          Alias Mark would be president
          if that could save some lives.'

'Wait. Wait. A crow should be prepared as follows:
throttle it, pay out a length of twine;
weight one end with a pebble, truss the talons,
sling it up and around a level branch;
            The same for clever kings, though they
            can be caught and trussed alive.'

        'You don't... you do not, you do NOT control'
'No?'
            'No! You didn't even know...'
                                            'We did
n't NEED to know, the detail, is for you,
the ignorant and innocent of creation.'
                                    'Did you create
            the heavens and the earth?'
                                    'We can't recall,

but fraught, intricate though it be, this plenum,
ground and stanza, was architect designed
(been blinded since: the man's a liability);
language, though anonymous, betrays
            the tact, resource, duplicity
            one's worst enemy might deploy.

Similarly, the world in its wisdom,
life as privilege, not some churl's right,
the invincible sway of the nucleus... are what we had
ordained. We ravel, render, rust and clone;
            it's true, we can't reboot
            the universe as yet, and yet

we reckon the likely answer is yes. We did it.'
            'Are you immortal? Or old as sand?'
            'Maybe: for when we need new blood,
membership and members, we co-opt
            or graft: these brown eyes
            see just as well as blue.'

'Who are you?'
                    'The guarantors of justice,
the governors.'

          'The arkhons!'
                    'The what?'
          I could have said excuse me, I'm drunk,
but no: I told them of the books
          two peasants in a dead land
          had lately brought to light.

'Written in a script obscure to modern thought,
on leaf long since extinct, bound in skin
of reptiles otherwise preserved in fossils;
handsome set, nine volumes, slightly foxed;
          made when immortality
          meant just that: it said "Who finds

the (blank) reality of these sayings will not
experience death." The arkhons moulded man
from clay they had divided, slip and slither,
from sky and the abyss, but woman was
          hidden from them as day from sleep,
          or as wisdom from the wind.

Och well if you can't create then legislate.
The rulers ruled you shall not we shall judge.
You shall not (text corrupt) not drink this cup.
Two duly did, got sent down for life.'
                              'Dereliction
          of duty! They broke the only
          law! Breach of trust!'

'The arkhons made man but they couldn't make him
live. That was some divine conspiracy,
though after their heinous crime the couple knew they
knew nothing, and that they would die (same thing):
          "This world consumes cadavers,
          while the truth subsists on life".'

'What are YOU, then: gullet or breath?'

'Eaten by truth.'

'And us?'

I grinned. 'Two brother bureaucrats
where I come from sold permits to build on rural
terrain. When one defected the other was caught.

One went on to great things
that overstrained his heart.

So the councillors had his brother hanged the morning
the long-haul frigid air connection left.
Well organised and cannibalised!' The dam-
age had been done. Great stone flags on the floor,

dark, clammy walls. In one
an iron rung was fixed.

The president was waiting. He took a solemn
tome; a voice came from him saying

'Do not
fear those who kill   the body, not the soul,
but him who can kill you   and put your soul in hell'.

All I could see there, in
the middle of the chamber; this

object, half pallet, half operating table.
Then we were back at meat. One of them burps
and yawns

'Transit, before you go, would you give us
a song?'

'What harbinger if I cried out would hear
or answer? Not that that
would stop me: you count on it.'

'Your granny.'

III

Don't go. Don't let the morning
turn your head with her shivering, thin grace,
in silk like a tarn that just forgot the starlight
before the sun takes its usual way with her.
     If dawn were a dove on the window ledge…
     but you don't want to know.

Don't go – all this in the dark, her lying there
like moonlight on the bed, like a memory,
beyond recall already, now the blackbirds
were telling the town what we had done that night,
     carving our initials
     on each other's hearts. They sang

Don't go – but the night was parcelled up in binbags.
You're on my mind so much, I hardly know
the noonday sun or frost in the bones of morning
And holy Joe the horseman telling folk
     he'd strip me bare as innocence
     and lead me back to the light

(relax, he'll never know I've let you in here);
the only man I ever hured with was him.
Goodbye: the yellow planets and the grey
dawn will attend you on your way. The sun
     will get around this blind. The sun
     will lever us apart.

I have her crouching at this square of canvas
quite naked. Black canvas. Black on white.
Heavy hair pinned up, and chin to cheekbone
mulled in light, like a pebble in the hand.
     She pulls the black aside –
     she rolls it up, we disappear.

– What was that, professor?
                                        – 'Twas an alba,
adjournment, 'the meeting rose at dawn'.
            – D'you think my mother wanted me to know that?
            – I've taught you all she wanted you to know.
            This was just to say – there's more
            than that. There's more than that.

            – Such as? What was all that stuff about the horseman?
            – Conflation with Hosea. Ask your priest:
I'd rather keep this secular… Such as:
leaving you at the grassy mountain pass,
            the moon on the hillside fragrant
            in the rags of the morning sun.

Wind of pollen from the full-blown lotuses
damp with drops of sweat from women's hair.
Scornfully last night she gave the traveller
straw for his bed; now at the dawn of day
            she takes it away, weeping
            (Rather try to stop the sun…)

With a rope I climbed into her coloured palace,
by firelight I climbed into her bed…
All you do is come to me, lie here awhile,
and then you go away and make me sad.
            The dawn appeared in darkness
            like a Yemenite sword unsheathed.

She longed to wake him, yet she loved to watch him.
Why should we rise because it is daylight?
Whoever lies with his love without concealment
(Did we lie down, because 'twas night?) can wait
            for day: your own sweet wedded wife
            can give such love as this.

In any event, love doesn't make you happy:
it makes you love.
                         – Who told you that?
                                        – No-one:
I read it in a book: Professor Hatto,
Eos (Mouton, The Hague) in sixty-five.
          I've been here nearly a year;
          it's time I went back to the wife.

          – You're married!
                         – Did I say that?
                                        – Don't play games with me.
          – I don't: I teach you games. That was the deal:
song, so folk can look and pretend they're listening,
lyrics you can use to hide your mouth –
          while music uses you. Play on
          until you get played out.

Imperatives that intersect in each of us,
overlapping clarities of speech,
economies where players come to pieces
in whose hands? There's violence in the game
          that nothing but its
          spiderweb conventions could contain –

not that they do.
                    – You have to go, then go
and tell my parents why.
                    – I can't.
                                   – Why not?
          – They won't believe me.
                                   – And should I?
                                        – No. Maybe.
Let me go.
          – Who's stopping you?
                                   – Then help
          me go.
                    – So who's the wife?
                    – I'll tell you. How about a drink?

Tantris, Tantris, stand at the embrasure
alone, until the sun go down, stressed and
strange. He's drinking red wine rough as a cat's lick.
His lute rests on a wolfskin; its head
     contingent with the stone floor.
     The fire gnaws its bones.

A Nubian vulture orbits like Mercator
over a ground of cinnamon and slate:
fifty below, at levels of abstraction
such that kin are motes in the eye; swim down,
     great imperial phosphorus,
     for the cooling warmth of blood

some never find, like a pebble that's been left
on a ledge, I'd lift and puddle in the sea,
the way you pick a poem from a bookshelf
and read it out. Go on: read this aloud
     and all the colours flush back,
     you remember you're alive

You.
     — I was a gyrovague.
                    — A what?
                            — A pilgrim.
     — Come off it.
                    — I was! The humblest man
in nation B. I was so poor and humble
that people came from miles around to see
     me in my cardboard box.
     They couldn't cope with it. And so

     – And so?
            – And so they made me metropolitan.
     – What's that?
            – A theocrat
               ?
                  – Don't ask.
I did quite well: the people came for council
or cure.
       – What did you cure them of?
                  – Don't know…
   snake bites, being ignored by
   sliding doors: that kind of thing.

This sky! As though the sun in its green stem
deployed such an astonishment of light
that stars and bolts beyond its purple tinges
came twirling in to the honeytrap…
                – Come on!
     – It was just like this one eve-
   ning I was called to the aerodrome.

Clearance cleared me, corridors propelled me
through the lumen of the catacomb
up and into terminal 4 – a hall all
glass, like a branch all bloom, that held the sky
      crimson lake. The amber
   in the fly. And in my eyes

I wanted to hold it just like that forever –
but then I thought Who is that in the green
silk skirt and jacket, midst the customs officers?
She looks so frail, sat slumped, feet set apart.
     I touched her hair. What face
   looked up to issue its command?

I apologised.
                    – What for?
                                        – For being there, or
for being late for touching her for not
being who she'd lifted her head in the hopes of seeing.
I looked down... silken slippers on her feet.
          'They don't sell shoes in airports
          and they don't wear them in hell.'

Try again. I knew that she'd been apprehended
in nothing but the clothes she wore, no papers but
an airport novel and chits from every duty-
free shop on the planet, some going back quite far.
          She hadn't clearly said where
          she was from or going to.

'What's the matter?'
                              'The uniforms maltreated me.'
'How?'
          'They came and took away my clothes.'
'They have to sometimes.'
                              The look she gave me
was made for those who'll never understand.
          The uniforms looked elsewhere.
          Last chance, I reckoned. Try again.

We happened to be sat across from an airport bar
(shut): bezelled gold on bottle-green glass sign,
THE SEPULCHRE: WINES AND SPIRITS. Crass ineptitude
or else it's homely plastic or *exotique*.
          'Why can't they just write Not Very
          Tasty Drink, Not Very Cheap?'

'They do that too', she said, 'It makes no difference:
it isn't read for real, it isn't read:
Credit is all that counts in virtuality;
mine just ran out.'
                              'Who were you travelling with?'
                    'A man I never thought I'd lose.'
Now this is the tale she told.

She said that, on account of some infraction –
tantric rites or serious taboo
(she wouldn't say) – she'd been down for a day in sheol,
and that was how she said she found herself
            locked in a women's prison
            on the slave coast. The screams

of women fighting, children frightened, losing
to cholera, cachexia
                        – What's that?
            – Look it up. One day and night, then some official
had her released; her man was out as well.
            He'd lost his tongue where he'd been.
            When the official asked Where to?

the answer dried in her throat. They were given visas
for different States, and that was what began
a journey there would never be an end to:
they wouldn't part and no one would admit
            the two of them together
            (even though their credit held).

From here to there, from north to south they travelled
wherever the wind would carry them. Not once
could they leave the transit areas, and never
were they alone. They never bedded down.
            They never heard a bird sing.
            They never felt the rain

except at times as they crossed the roaring concrete
to board another plane. He took to drink
(osmosis, he explained, the drink remembered
what he forgot). Well one thing he forgot
            was her passport in a previous
            continent. He went back to fetch it.

— And didn't come back?

                         — Forgot where he was going,
got robbed or rearrested. Who's to say?
I tried to arrange provisional asylum
till his return at least. And that was where
        I had a serious run-in
        with my own superiors.

You see I'd taken all her talk of sheol
as mild derangement from her stint in gaol,
best repaired by restoring her companion,
the only point of reference in her life.
        My colleagues deemed she *was*
        in hell and couldn't leave *because*

the woman had no other point of reference:
the pair of them was long past praying for.
They packed her off on a plane for god knows only.
We're all dry wi drinkin o't, we're dry,
        The parson kissed the fiddler's wife
        and he couldny sleep for thinkin o't.

It wasn't long till I got my marching orders,
promotion sideways, to a silent see.
For just like the lunar mapping litany, MARE
SERENITATIS, MARE IMBRIUM,
        the kirk carves up the planet
        in celestial fantasy.

I got the Tantum Erg Orientalis
on vellum — it was off the edge of the map
with footnotes from a Portuguese *roteiro*
on what to do when the horses all collapsed.
        They expected me to step down,
        but I took it. What the hell.

The journey? You wouldn't believe me if I told you.
　　　　– I don't believe you.
　　　　　　　　　　　　– Told you! There I was
fucked and far from home (I beg your pardon:
I shouldn't drink this stuff at the full moon)
　　　　　so I set to making prayer wheels,
　　　　　mine-detectors, alphabets.

It was a place of no machine technology
but some sophistication, not to say
corruption. O why not? Let's say corruption.
Corruption! bribe and bully, buy and sell.
　　　　　The cardboard box or local equivalent
　　　　　was my selling point.

Whatever I had or made I gave or bartered
for beans or company. I did make friends.
I couldn't cure a soul of any illness;
when I took sick, though, they looked after me.
　　　　　Some were as good as anyone
　　　　　could be without belief.

I made myself such a mandorla of poverty
that once, when I was held up by mistake,
the robber recognising me apologised
and gave me some loose change to buy a cake.
　　　　　He thought I'd never seen one.

He asked me though to tell my next-door neighbour
that if he didn't pay up he was dead.
I asked him what the problem was, he said please
just tell him. I told him, he went nuts.
　　　　　Don't eat the prayer wheel, Charlie,
　　　　　I only finished it yesterday.

It turned out Charlie had a gambling problem.
Three gambling problems: (1) he never won,
(2) the hoodlums that he never won to,
(3) no money. They would settle for
　　　　　(a) his head or (b) his son;
　　　　　I said I'd pay them off.

What else could I do? That joker swore by his family
that never would he look at cards again.
People lost their time for me: directly
or indirectly I worked for The Men.
        The only one who seemed
        to understand me was his wife.

– You loved her?
             – Who said anything about loving,
Exult? She talked to me, I talked to her.
Her husband, though, maybe thought that there was more to it;
he decided he would have to win her back
        by clearing his debt to me,
        by winning all that money back.

I think he must have borrowed from the rival
banking clan, with me as guarantee.
The upshot was I found myself indentured
twice. The night he lost, I went to say
        goodbye to his woman. She said
        But you wouldn't leave me here?

     – You took her?
             – I took her along.
                    – You bastard!
And what about her children?
             – What about them?
   – You mean you worked your way into their confidence
then stole the one they all depended on?
        – I didn't steal, I gave.
     I gave them all I had and more.

– Giving more than you have is the same as stealing.
    – It says Sell what you have and give to the poor:
I did that. It was not enough. And no one
did rescue or redeem me. I tried.
    I screwed up. Like the gambler.
    Like his woman.
                        – What'll you do?

    – Go back.
                    – To Tantum Erg?
                                – No, no, to Tintagel,
I mean to Nation B. The lady wife
awaits. My dinner's getting cold.
                            – The others?
    – Look, I don't know, and even if I did
what's done is done. You can't condemn
me if you didn't help.

In any case I know that there's forgiveness
for all of this.
                – Whoever told you that?
    – No one. It was punched on a roll of paper
that fed the pneumatic organ in a kirk
    I helped refurbish after we'd
    got back to Nation B.

The theme came out in a voice like uillean bagpipes
The rest was as though mallets wrapped in felt
addressed a glockenspiel. It was in F minor
like light among the liftshafts of the beech
        trees in a nameless forest.
        The opening gambit wasn't new:

it dropped from C to F along a handspan
and worked its way back up with a show of skill.
Aiming to move on up it got to E flat
but the harmony wasn't providing air support
        there was something out of orbit
        a muted solemn carousel.

I checked the roll but it was turning smoothly
the piping tune subsided to A flat
the glockenspiel got back in gear, but thenceforth,
however brave, the anthem sounded frail
        anxious, regretful, and yet... consoled.
                – Was that it?

                            – That was it.

NOTES

Town Shanties

'Novodevichi': Vladimir Solovyov and his sister, Allegra, are buried in the monastery grounds.

'Augrim' follows a visit to Chartres cathedral.

'Six Rehabs': These are from a series of eighteen poems, counting the originals. I began with a rehab of a famous poem, and Edwin Morgan countered with a reconstruction of same. Our versions first appeared in *Verse*; the reconstructions have since been republished in *Themes on a Variation*. All eighteen texts are archived on www.knot.ch.

'Rehab No. 6': Decus et tutamen. The legend on the English pound coin, meaning 'comely and protective', was the description of a coat of mail Aeneas awarded a boatman in the Aeneid.

The ancient Harappan inscription, transcription and translation are quoted from an article in *Scientific American*.

Thunderstone: stone arrowheads, from even earlier times, were later thought to be the residue of thunderbolts.

'Sous les pavés – la plage': it seems that when the students of Paris howked up cobblestones to make barricades in 1968 they found a layer of sand underneath. They took this as a sign: dismantle civilisation and life becomes idyllic.

'Libation Theology': Anopheles is the malarial mosquito; the quotation is Webster's definition of 'prester'; Prester John was to European empires what Santa Claus was to Christmas.

'Not Being Bob De Niro': refers to a feature that appeared in a *Sunday Observer* colour supplement in summer 1987.

'Cradle': the first two thirds of part II is taken almost verbatim from an article by Michael White in *The Guardian*, 13 November 1987.

For What It Is, a poem co-written with Alan Riach, appeared originally in *Edinburgh Review* and was republished separately by Untold Books (Christchurch, New Zealand). My thanks to Alan, the joint copyright holder, for permission to reproduce these excerpts.

Dhow was once 'The Flyting of Kennedy and Dunbar'.

In the Metaforest

'Arjuna and Draupadi in Glasgow' was written after I had seen Peter Brook's Mahabharata there.

'Chemin de la Riole' is my path home from work. That evening, there was a warm, sand-laden rain that had crossed the sea and the Alps from North Africa. Neutrinos, which the second stanza talks about, were postulated by Enrico Fermi in the 1930s – the time of Mandelstam's

'Slate Ode', MacDiarmid's 'On a Raised Beach' and other inhuman events – but no collisions with other particles were detected for some time, since they pour clean through the world like rain through air; some detectors have been set in ocean trenches, where the dark is deep and the decay of a neutrino could be noticed. For the story of Dido and Aeneas, which recurs in one of the India poems, see Virgil's Aeneid, Book IV.

'GVA': the airline code for Geneva. Mont Jallouvre, visible from the centre of town, dominates the plateau de Glières, a centre of resistance during the Second World War, crushed when the Nazis sent in gliders. Switzerland was neutral.

'Whereas it's better...' owes something to the last stanza of Emily Dickinson's '"Arcturus" is his other name' (no. 70 of the Complete Poems).

'What'll it be now, Patrick?': 'Patrick' is Patrick Bowles, a colleague who translated Molloy with Samuel Beckett.

'The sky was the usual southern mess': the candlepod acacia is a hollow thorn bush, in which lions rest when the sun is high.

'Sophia' is Divine Wisdom.

'Paludrine': malaria began MacDiarmid's poetic career and ended Dante's.

'Strangler Fig': Les Murray has a less diffuse poem on the same plant.

'Tristia' is drawn from the conversation of a friend who was worried about her daughter working in Abkhazia. Phoolan Devi (otherwise quite beside the point) cropped up in the conversation: she had been released from prison in India, pardoned for a series of revenge killings.

'Artou' was a map and travel guide shop in Geneva.

'Due to this earth quake hit' comes from a letter received by the 1% for Development Fund. A lakh is 100,000.

'From the Metaforest' is drawn from Paul Deussen, The Philosophy of the Upanishads, translated by A.S. Geden, 1906, reprinted New York, Dover, 1966.

'On Reading John Berryman's "Eleven Addresses to the Lord"': John Berryman in his Dream Songs uses an alter ego named Henry Bones. The names, and the theme of conversion in his Addresses to the Lord, recalled John Henry, Cardinal Newman.

'Presto!': Partick is in Glasgow's West End, Bridgeton in the East End.

A4ism: for 'theism' see Chambers. You wouldn't believe it if you read it here.

Tantris

Based on an episode from Gottfried von Strassburg's unfinished epic on Tristan and Isolde; I used the translation by A.T. Hatto (Penguin Classics).

While I was working on it, Pléiade issued a volume containing all the major mediaeval texts, including Sir Tristrem, edited by Walter Scott, who liked to think that its author was Thomas of Ercildoune, Thomas the Rhymer (who turns up in 'In the Metaforest'). It wasn't the Scottish connection that interested me so much as the idea of a stranger at the point of death who's making himself up as he goes along, and who has to leave before he is finally caught out. The subject allowed me to tackle art, politics and religion; each part centres on stories of people I know (Parts I and III) or know of (Part II). It's all happened; it's still happening.